Recipes for Disaster

Recipes for Disaster

A Memoir

Tess Rafferty

Thomas Dunne Books ≈ St. Martin's Press
New York

I like to drink. The events in this memoir happened as written to the best of my memory, but as they all involve alcohol, one or two details might be off. If you're reading this book thinking, "That didn't happen that way! I was there!" well then, may I remind you that you were probably drinking, too. Also, some of the names and identifying characteristics have been changed so as to protect the privacy of those involved and not cause further issues at my next dinner party.

THOMAS DUNNE BOOKS.
An imprint of St. Martin's Press.

www.thomasdunnebooks.com
www.stmartins.com

Design by Anna Gorovoy

Rafferty, Tess.
    Recipes for disaster : a memoir / by Tess Rafferty.—1st ed.
        p. cm.
    ISBN 978-1-250-01143-5 (hardcover)
    ISBN 978-1-250-01834-2 (e-book)
    1. Dinners and dining.   2. Dinners and dining—Humor.   3. Entertaining. 4. Entertaining—Humor.   5. Cooking.   6. Cooking—Humor.   7. Rafferty, Tess.   I. Title.
    TX737.R244 2012
    642—dc23

                                                                    2012033164

First Edition: November 2012

10   9   8   7   6   5   4   3   2   1

To my grandparents, Mike and Mary Rose, who first introduced me to the idea that good food could be enjoyed in the midst of great drama.

To Frank and Knoxie, who helped to develop my love of sharing good meals.

And to Chris, who gives me someone to share these meals—and my life—with.

Contents

Acknowledgments

I am extremely grateful to so many people who helped make this book a reality, in ways both direct and indirect. First of all, to my agent Holly Root, who always believed in my writing and was an endless source of help and handholding as we honed this idea and made it work. And to my lawyer, Chad Christopher, who brought Holly into my life when I said I needed a book agent.

To *The Soup* writing staff, Lee Farber, Nic DeLeo, Andrew Genser, Greg Fideler, Darren Belitsky, and Jonah Ray who endured more than one writers' dinner at my house and to our chief, K.P. Anderson who was always understanding and gave me the time to work on this when I needed to write. And to the world's best clip show jockey, Joel McHale, for his enthusiastic support of this project.

To Christy Stratton Mann and Alex Alexander who participated in the Girls' Cooking Club experiments, which first gave me the idea that I might have something to say about entertaining.

To Matthew Taylor for drawing the awesome Flaming Weenie Tree.

To my talented friends who orchestrated an amazing cover shoot when I called them in a panic: art director Gary Kordan, photographer Justine Ungaro, and makeup artist David Marvel.

To everyone who provided early support for this book: Cathryn Michon, Adena Halpern, Deborah Vankin, and Whitney Cummings.

To all of my agents at Paradigm: Doug Fronk, Chris Licata, Jana Marimpietri, Shawn Scallon, and Ida Ziniti, as well as to Johnathan Berry at 3 Arts, for all of their enthusiasm for this project.

And to my father, who taught me how to make veal paprikash, and my mother, who was never much of a cook, but was a voracious reader and always let me read at the dinner table, thus instilling the other passion necessary in the writing of this book.

And of course, warmest thanks to Chris McGuire, who selflessly lets his life be turned upside down whenever I get one of my bright ideas. Thank you for doing the dishes, cooking breakfast, and getting the cat off my papers while I completed the edits, Sweetie!

The meals . . . were designed to prolong our time together; the food was of course meant to nourish us, but it was also meant to satisfy, in some deeper way, our endless hunger for one another.

—*Passion on the Vine* by Sergio Esposito

Recipes for Disaster

prologue

"I am an onion," I think to myself.

It sounds like one of those bullshit acting exercises I once paid tens of thousands of dollars to learn how to do instead of learning how to actually act. But instead of taking me back to a time when I was told that character could be achieved if I just learned how to effectively breathe out of my rectum, I think it again. "I am an onion."

Maybe I should start at the beginning. In the beginning there was no onion. In the beginning there was only the question:

"Why am I doing this?"

This is what I'm thinking as I crush up fresh basil and mint to flavor pitchers of water for that evening's dinner. I am cooking dinner for twelve people: one person can't eat gluten, two people are lactose intolerant, one woman only eats chicken and fish, and another I have just found out is vegetarian, despite the fact that I served her boeuf bourguignon in my house just six months ago. Also, my throat closes if I have any fruit and many vegetables, but this is at least a challenge I am used to.

"Seriously," I ask myself, "why do I do this?"

It is not a resentful question. I am not angry at a lack of appreciation I have projected onto guests who haven't even arrived yet, nor do I feel stressed out and rushed. I am neither of those things as I have learned through endless trials and miserable errors the secrets to serving a hot meal while making sure that things don't get so stressful that I melt down. At least I think I have. As the night will prove, sometimes no matter how calm you remain, twelve iPhones in a room will interfere with your boyfriend's wireless sound system and somehow your night will end with a fight and tears at two in the morning.

But I am getting ahead of myself. At this moment in time I do not know that I will be sleeping in the spare room tonight and I have allowed the entire day to prepare for this dinner party. Which again makes me ask, "Why? Why does it seem perfectly reasonable to me to spend an entire day two weeks before Christmas working on a dinner that is not even the last one I will be cooking this season? Why am I flavoring water, when most people don't even care about the wine we're drinking?"

The question is detached from all emotion. I am generally curious about what makes me do this, like I am my own science experiment. And the only answer I can come up with is, "I guess I must like it."

When I think back on it, I have wanted to throw dinner parties since I was in high school. The night the fall play opened junior year, I thought it would be fun to have a select group of the cast over for dinner before our call time. We made fettuccine Alfredo because My On-Again Off-Again Boyfriend (aka Future Gay Best Friend) said he wanted to eat pasta to give him more energy during the show, like it was a marathon and not *You're a Good Man, Charlie Brown*. Looking back, it seems really odd that my instinct as a re-bellious Goth teen was to suddenly get all Martha Stewart rather than go drink in a parking lot somewhere; however, it's prescient of a comment The Boyfriend made just a few years ago, "You'd rather throw a dinner party than work on your career."

That is not true—entirely. I think I throw dinner parties so that I *can* work on my career without putting a gun in my mouth. I'd much rather put fresh pasta and a Brunello in there. (Hmmm... I'm getting notes of gunpowder and des-peration.) More importantly, cooking a meal and entertain-ing is a project that has a physical outcome that you can see and taste and touch. Working on your career is a project that has no beginning, middle, or end and, often, no out-come. But setting a table is a creative endeavor that has to live up to no one's expectations but my own. I don't get "notes" on where I placed the silverware or told that my flower arrange-ment appeals to the wrong demographic. Preparing food is a meditation. And I get to make something delicious the way I want to make it, and as long as I follow some simple steps it will all turn out perfectly.

OK, sometimes the food sucks. Sometimes no matter how many times you've made it before, some weird atmo-spheric condition occurs or maybe you just weren't paying attention to how much salt you used and the whole thing blows up in your face and you have to serve someone beef that never tenderized or maybe a runny polenta. And it's the worst kind of rejection because every other kind of rejection is subjective; just because someone didn't like your screenplay doesn't mean it wasn't good. But when you don't like your own food, there's no shrugging it off with "that person's a hack who hasn't produced a hit ever." I am not a hack and as far as dinner has gone, I've produced many hits.

And what's worse—you have to still eat it.

Cookbooks should have a whole chapter on dealing with disappointment. Or they should be written by actors and writers because we deal with disappointment every day. And as much as feeling disappointment pains you, it's probably the flip side of what allows you to enjoy your creation so much. Cooks who don't feel disappointment probably don't realize when their food is bad so they probably don't feel exhilarated when it's good, either.

So maybe the question isn't, "Why do I do this?" but "Why do I like it?" Why do I love something that is so much work, that doesn't make me money, but rather often costs me hundreds of dollars in things like truffle honey and Le Creuset pots, and that can often end in disappointment? Food is about celebrating the present. When you're eating good food, you're totally in the moment, experiencing all the flavors of both the food and the company in front of you. When you use your good dishes and set a gorgeous table, you're really saying, "This moment is going to be beautiful because it's the only one there is." I am not going to focus on the fact that the flowers will die tomorrow or tell myself the china is only for special occasions, because today is a special occasion and we never know when we might go the way of the flowers.

Recently, I was cutting an onion and I noticed that the grain of the onion—the lines that run from stem to stem—

went sideways. On one side it started straight, but then it started listing to one side, like some graph of a complicated calculus problem that I never could grasp, but decided it didn't matter because I was going to be an actress anyway. I couldn't stop staring at the imperfection; it looked so cool. It was so unusual. And that's when I realized nature wasn't perfect, either. Here I was trying to cook the perfect dinner, when even my ingredients weren't perfect. They were interesting, to be sure, and different, but not perfect. And yet, that onion wasn't beating itself up and feeling like a failure. It was still an onion.

My dinners aren't perfect. But they are interesting and unusual and different. And through it all I may have finally learned to be happy when my grain grows in another direction. I am still an onion.

Chapter 1
How to Cook a Turkey,
or The Stomach:
Not the Way to a Man's Pants

The final Thanksgiving I spent with my family my father said grace. We were not a religious family, despite the fact that we had all done some time in Catholic school. Sure, we had gone to church weekly when we were kids, but it became more sporadic as we got older. We had First Communions, mostly because we were Italian and when you're Italian, that's your first fund-raiser. But we never heard righteous treacle like, "God has this in his plan for you," and for that I will always be grateful to my parents.

I don't remember us saying grace much, if ever, which is why it was so strange when my father said, "Dear Lord, we would like to thank you for everything you've given us. We have one child who smokes and another who's been kicked out of school, but at least we have each other, Lord, although sometimes that's not much of a consolation."

It was my freshman year of college. I hadn't been planning to come home at all, but at the last minute I found myself both missing my boyfriend and cooling on the friend at whose house I had been planning to spend the weekend. So I came home with my friend Erin in tow.

My grandmother had been the cook in the family and after she died three years prior, Thanksgiving became a rather forgettable holiday. Her amazing stuffing had been replaced with Stove Top. We stopped spending the holiday with our cousins, aunts, and uncles and as my father has already mentioned, he and my mother and my brother and I weren't much consolation to each other. So after that first Thanksgiving home, I decided that I had no compelling reason to go home for that again, certainly not with Christmas a mere four weeks later. I wonder now if my grandmother had lived longer—or if my mother or her siblings had been able to continue the culinary tradition—if that would have changed things. After all, people who go home regularly for holidays usually talk about how they can't wait for a favorite aunt's pie or their mother's sweet potatoes, and their travel experiences and family dynamics must be just as difficult as mine have always been. Maybe it's the food that keeps you coming back. I've been known to put up with a lot of bullshit in order to eat some truly delicious food. I never turn down an opportunity to eat at Osteria Mozza even though I'm certain child molesters on death row are served their last meal with less attitude. Bad service, condescending friends, judgmental siblings . . . isn't it all the same thing?

So, the following year, Thanksgiving away from home,

while fun, wasn't much of a culinary adventure. Erin and I spent the holiday in Boston, eating canned vegetables and watching *Moonlighting* reruns on an obscure cable channel. The year after was too much of one. I found myself in Prague with my roommate: two girls alone who had just walked into a gigantic beer hall of an establishment, filled only with men. The tables ran the length of the room and had benches instead of chairs; what we now refer to charmingly as family style, but in that moment felt more like "gang rape" than "family." They made room for us at a table and instead of having their way with us, just handed us menus written entirely in Czech. Fortunately, we were sitting by the one man who spoke a small amount of English, enough to point to one item on the menu that was "chicken and Camembert." It was simple but good, much better than we expected and we went back again the next night.

The following year I decided to cook. For the first time I was living alone, in what felt like a spacious one-bedroom apartment, one floor beneath a roof deck. It was about five hundred square feet and the last flight of stairs was so old and crooked it felt like they performed back-alley abortions at the top. The only heat in the apartment was on the side of the stove. It was a pipe, punctured with many small holes and encased in a metal box. Periodically the pipe would fill with gas and then the pilot would light it so that what was heating your house was nothing more than a pipe with flames coming out of it. The heat would cause the metal case to expand and then about five minutes after the heat shut off, it would snap back into its original place with a THANG! All night you would hear this cycle as you tried to sleep: the hiss of natural gas filling your apartment, the THWOOOOSH as the entire pipe caught fire, and then, once you finally started to get back to sleep, the metallic THANG of the metal contracting, the whole time thinking it was a distinct possibility you would never live to see the morning.

My apartment was in the North End of Boston, the quaint Italian section of town that had not yet been touched by high-end condos and supermarket chains. Every day I would walk home past Polcari's, the spice store run by the ancient brother and sister who sold spices by the ounce in little paper bags for fifty cents. They had whole coffee beans, an assortment of rice and flours, and the best price on chocolate-covered espresso beans anywhere in the city. Across the street was Bova's bakery, which was open twenty-four hours a day, because someone was always inside baking bread. No matter what time of the night I was coming home, I could always get fresh bread, usually still hot from the oven, and my friends and I would plunge our drunken fists into the center and pull out chunks of the warm, white fluff. There were a couple of different butcher shops, a few produce markets, a liquor store. There were numerous pastry shops and every Easter they'd have cakes shaped like lambs with white coconut frosting in the window. It sounds totally garish, but I loved them because I remembered seeing them every Easter dinner as a little girl. Right before I turned down my street was the "Boston I," the closest thing they had to a grocery store. It reminded me of the market my grandmother had gone to while I was growing up. They sold deli meats in the back and the shelves were stacked with pasta and soups and necessities. That was a family-run business, too, and as I never had an extra key, if I had to make sure a friend needed to get into my apartment, I left it with Chuckie or Cheryl behind the counter. I could walk home every day and do my shopping as I went; talk to Miss Polcari about what to do with cream of tartar, ask the butcher what looked good, get a little local gossip.

Maybe it was the inspiration I found daily at the markets or the nostalgia inducing lamb cakes that made me want to cook that year. But most likely, it was Simon.

Simon was in my ballet class freshman year. I was a savvy enough freshman to know that men in your (elective) ballet class weren't good crush material, and I still held onto this notion long after I learned (to my surprise) that Simon was straight. The next semester he was in my jazz dance class. He was a handsome, skinny guy with longish hair, always in a sleeveless black T-shirt and black bike shorts, two earrings and no smile. The summer after jazz class, we found ourselves taking the same extracurricular acting class from a teacher we both loved who had his own studio. The work was entirely movement based and it was another opportunity for Simon to wear his jazz/ballet ensemble. Eventually we had a Shakespeare class together and I finally got to see him in pants. By this time I knew he had a girlfriend who was a year ahead of me and they felt practically married. He seemed like one of those people who took "the work" very seriously, whatever work, whether it was ballet, jazz, Shakespeare, or bartending. I didn't trust people like that as I was afraid if I took anything that seriously I could still fail and then what?

Despite our increasing number of classes together we didn't become friends until he and his girlfriend broke up. Not that it was romantic; I just think when they were no longer together he was forced to open up his world a bit, especially as they had had so many friends in common. I was going through something of a breakup, too, having had a falling out with my roommate of three years. The timing was right: we both needed a new friend.

I remember exactly when it shifted. We were in Shakespeare class together, tying our shoes after getting into our Elizabethan garb and he said, "You're going to call me this summer, right, Tess?"

I was shocked that he wanted to be my friend. Sure, after three years of ballet tights, iambic pentameter, and crawling across the floor pretending to be prehistoric protozoa, we had finally relaxed a bit and started to actually make each other laugh. But now this once standoffish person who it took me three years to get comfortable with wanted to actually be my friend outside of school, like real friends. Not just the fake kind who pretend to like each other in class because their girlfriend of three years dumped them and they have no one else to talk to.

I assured him I would call him, and so I did, getting his voice-mail each and every time. Simon never called back. Finally, I called, he didn't answer, and so I left my last message. "Hi, Simon, it's Tess. I only take this shit from guys I sleep with. Call me back." He did that day, laughing.

He was a few years older than the rest of us and had friends and experiences and a life outside of our college, which was one of the reasons I liked being his friend. He had a perspective that most other people I knew lacked, and also, a determination; having been on his own since sixteen, he worked as a bartender three or four nights a week until two in the morning to pay for school. I saw myself in him, or at least wanted to. Since I had gotten back from Europe the year before, I felt stifled; my world had once again been limited to the lives and dramas of people in a four-block radius. When you're staring at the Colosseum, it's kind of hard to think that who got the lead in the Sondheim musical is going to matter in two thousand years. I returned to Boston with a desire to work hard, study hard, and achieve great things. And now one of these great things I wanted to achieve was having sex with Simon.

It started in the fall. We had both been cast in an obscure German play written by a man who spent his entire life looking for the perfect woman to commit suicide with. The director of our play was a crazy Dutchman, who had an Italian name and only one testicle, which for some reason I knew about. As would become a pattern in my life, my relationship with Simon developed over food.

Every night before class we would meet for dinner. I was always on my way back to campus from work and he was coming from class and neither one of us had time to return home to eat. It became a ritual, both of us just showing up at the acting studio each night. He'd put his arm around me and I'd say, "Are we dining?" He'd say, "Yes," and off we would go to spend an entire hour's worth of retail pay on a fancy Back Bay sandwich just so we could talk. And one of these days as he was talking, his voice soft and raspy due to damage during childhood surgery, there was something about the combination of his words and the look on his face. I looked at him and was overwhelmed with the urge to say, "I like you."

What I didn't like was the sandwich I was having that night. Something didn't taste right about it and I was worried that I was having some sort of an allergic reaction. Simon was doing most of the talking at this point, and didn't seem at all worried that I might be turning blue or puffing up at any moment. But when we got up to leave he saw that my sandwich was mostly untouched. He took a moment to wrap it up and said, "I vomited so much of my own neurosis onto the table, there wasn't any room for your sandwich." These were the most romantic words I had heard to date!

After rehearsal that night, we went with the rest of the cast for drinks and Crazy Dutch Director with Italian Name came with us. The two beers I had on my non-sandwich-filled stomach left me feeling pretty buzzed (Oh, for the days when I had no tolerance!) and in no position to react well when Crazy Dutch Director asked me why I was so bitter. Um, maybe because crazy, foreign, one-balled men who should be old enough to know better buy me drinks and then insult me? Despite Simon coming to my defense, I felt awkward and self-conscious so naturally, Simon and I go back to the Mad Dutchman's house for bourbon. I don't drink bourbon.

I was drunk on my ability to have an opinion. He was drunk on his delusions of Svengaliism. We were both drunk on bourbon. What followed was the interrogation of a mouthy, idealstic college girl armed with way too much reading, by a man with one testicle and English as a second language. At one point he tells me to, "Go into politics then, don't be an actor!" At another he says, "I ask you questions and you respond with tears." At another, I am on his lap and he is drying my tears. It was around this point that Simon tells me we have to go. Good call. He takes me back to his place, gives me water and goldfish crackers to "slow the alcohol down from reaching the liver." (Does this actually work?)

The two of us pass out platonically on his bed as the sun comes up. I loved this man!

The next morning we tried to make sense of the bizarre evening and he says to me, "I want you to know, Tess, if I had thought you were in any danger, I would have had you out of there, if I didn't think it was safe." I so loved this man!

October rehearsals gave way to November and as that month started to slip away and we drew closer to opening night, I knew I was nearing the end of my daily excuse to see Simon. Determined to take our relationship to the next level, I formulated a plan. I needed to create an opportunity to spend more time with him; time when he didn't have to take off for his 10 p.m. shift at the club. I would have to cook Thanksgiving dinner. Wasn't it the same with Peppermint Patty and Charlie Brown? Doesn't she invite herself over to Thanksgiving dinner because she has such a crush on him?

Rounding out my guest list was one of my best friends, Anna, a grad student in literature; her very English boyfriend, Nigel; the very opinionated Regina who was on her third year as a senior; and my brother, the drummer, Junior.

Junior was in his first year at the Berklee College of Music, also in Boston. I had been excited that he was going to school in the same town I was and had visions of us hanging out and going to concerts together. As it turned out, *he* went out and *he* went to concerts. *I* stayed home and tried to reach him and *I* worried.

I was predisposed to worry about him ever since the time I was five and he was three and we were playing at my grandmother's house. My mother walked into the room and started freaking out. This was not uncommon. The reason, however, was. My brother had eaten some of my mother's cigarettes. Later he would learn that not only could they be smoked, you could actually smoke stuff better than cigarettes. And then one day still later, I would see him eat that, too. But that day he was just eating cigarettes.

My mother looked at me. "Why weren't you watching him?"

Looking back now, I realize the answers to that question were the following: a) not my son, b) not my cigarettes, and c) I'm five.

But at the time I just thought, "Oh, I guess that's my job," and the role of the overprotective older sibling was forged.

His first week of school he called me at work to find out how to get to Providence, Rhode Island, by train. He didn't know anyone in Providence; he didn't know anyone in Boston yet. I told him to take the commuter rail and tried to give him all the information I could before I had to get back to work. I worried the rest of the shift. Would he know to get back before the trains stopped running? Would he not get himself mugged or arrested? He'd had his first run-in with the law that summer for misdemeanor jackassery, which had gotten plea-bargained down to first degree being a stoner, but I didn't know if he'd be as lucky in a town where his lawyer wouldn't be a friend of my father's who normally handled high-profile murder cases. And exactly why again was he going to Providence? As soon as I got off work, I tried to call him back. And I kept trying for the next twenty-four hours. What would he do if he missed that last train? Would he try to hitchhike? Would he try to sleep in the park? When he finally picks up, he tells me that he spent the night in Providence ... in Cheap Trick's hotel suite.

My first thought is what exactly did my brother do to get

into Cheap Trick's hotel suite. But then he explains one of the band members has a kid who played soccer with a friend of my brother's at Berklee and so they all went down to Providence to see them play. My brother wasn't performing untoward acts to get backstage, he was actually hanging with someone's dad.

Another night I had gotten home rather late to find my door open. I had given my brother a key in case he ever needed to come by, but still, that was no reason he should leave the door wide open. I found him "asleep" on a haphazardly pulled out futon that had one whole half pulled up onto a trunk. I panicked as it got increasingly harder to wake him up and when I finally did I noticed his T-shirt was smeared with blood.

Still another time, he shows up at night, sunglasses still on, talking about the ride in. "It was bedlam on the bus, man." Just then he reaches inside his jean jacket and pulls out a plastic cup of beer from his inside pocket, like some deadbeat James Bond.

With all the worrying I was doing about my brother, my love life, and crazy Dutch directors, it's probably little wonder that I had also just started suffering from acid reflux, a condition that would haunt my red-wine loving, foodie soul for years to come. Only I didn't quite know what it was at the time. I only knew I was experiencing intense chest and back pain on a regular basis and was convinced I had a lung collapsing. The pain was most severe across my back so I had asked my brother to show up around one that afternoon to help me get the large turkey into the oven.

I wasn't starting the turkey until early afternoon because I didn't intend to eat until eight that night. I think eating a large meal at two o'clock in the afternoon is completely weird and unnatural, like putting a TV set outdoors so you can watch TV from your pool.

One o'clock came and went and no brother. I tried calling. He didn't answer. Shocker. Rather than tell him I only take this from guys I sleep with, I put the turkey in the oven myself. I followed the simple steps my father had given me the day before: wash out the turkey, and take out the neck and bag of giblets. I only found a bag with the neck in it and I was pretty thorough so I figured some turkey along the line must have had two bags of giblets or something. I poured butter over it, stuck a thermometer into what I thought was the thickest part of the thigh without touching bone, although fuck if I knew. Every time I tried to keep it from touching bone, it just ended up coming out the other side of the leg. I tried to push it down as far as I could without touching the bone, but how do I know where that is? Eventually, I did the best I could and away it went into the oven, covered with aluminum foil.

During all of this, my brother didn't call, but Simon did. We talked for long enough that he invited me over his place to hang before dinner.

"Umm . . . you mean the dinner that I'm cooking? That I have a bird in the oven right now for. . . . But you can come over here early, if you want."

Now we had the whole afternoon to hang before any of my cockblocking friends got there! Or my prodigal brother. If he wasn't dead.

I had asked Simon to bring the wine since he was a bartender and would know about such things and also since he was over twenty-one. He arrived in his uniform: jeans, black turtleneck, black John Fluevogs. He took off his long coat; he was cold and smelled like winter. On the table was the brown bag of wine. I looked inside to take the wine out and I saw what looked like a condom in there. Not used or anything. Wrapped. He wasn't a weirdo.

I don't ask myself the following questions:

- Why would a man wander the streets of Boston on Thanksgiving, carrying one lone condom in a bag when he has a wallet, a coat, and jeans?

- Why would he leave it in the paper bag with the wine, after I've said, "Let me get the wine?"

- Who's going to baste the turkey every hour if I'm in the bedroom letting Simon stuff my cavity?

But he doesn't stuff my cavity. Instead we spend the afternoon talking and eventually other friends arrive. Regina comes with a selection of sides from Boston Market. I am horrified, but impressed by her effort as she hates to cook and this, to her, is cooking. Anna and Nigel show up. She with a chocolate trifle; he with a foreigner's skepticism about our American holiday. Still no brother, but Simon is touching me, putting his arm around me, which more than makes up for Junior's disappearance.

I had invited one other person, my friend Samantha, an ethereal redhead who women wanted to be and men wanted to sleep with. She was a deep, old soul who could talk to you like you were the only one in the world who understood her and she, you. She was also notoriously fucking unreliable. The calls had started that morning.

"I'm coming. I'm coming. I just need to take a nap."

"I'm so sorry. I fell asleep for longer than I thought. But I'm coming."

"Definitely. But I may be a little late."

So I had two guests MIA, another I was trying to seduce, and the mashed potatoes needed to be started. This was my first lesson in what a goddamn pain mashed potatoes were. They're almost impossible to do ahead of time. Oh, I've read the tips, too. "Simply reheat with some more milk and butter." "Reheat in the oven." "Keep warm in the crockpot." They just don't taste right. And cooking them at dinner time is a military operation. All you want to do is eat and these fuckers have to be peeled and then cut and then boiled and then mashed. All while you're trying to make gravy. Which it was also time to start.

I was proud of my first turkey, so far. The basting had worked and I had plenty of pan drippings to make my gravy with, which everyone knows is the whole point. Turkey merely exists as a surface to help you shovel gravy into your mouth. Only something happened while I was pulling the cooked turkey out of the pan. A brown, plastic bag fell out. I didn't get a turkey without giblets, after all; instead the plastic bag must have been wedged so far inside of it, I couldn't find it. And now I had just cooked said plastic bag at 325°F for seven hours. That couldn't be good.

Concerned, I called my friend Steve, a chef. I also called my brother once for good measure. Still no answer. But Steve picked up.

"Steve! Help! I cooked the turkey with the bag of giblets in it!"

"All right," he said in his laid back, deadhead fashion. "You are going to have some awesome gravy, then."

Steve assured me that everyone does this at least once. Convinced I'm not going to kill anyone, I turned my attention back to the potatoes and the gravy. Lively discussion drifted in from the next room. The kind of discussion I couldn't wait to get out of high school to have and that I now long for when I'm being forced to listen to what everyone is wearing to Mommy & Me class. Regina and Nigel are discussing German poetry. This is exactly the sort of French salon I imagined would happen at my first Thanksgiving when I pushed those two steamer trunks together that afternoon and used an Indian tapestry as a tablecloth.

The phone rings. It's not my brother. It's Samantha.

"I'm coming, but please start without me. I don't mind. I just can't motivate to leave right now."

She was in the strange German play with us, too, only she was the lead and was carrying on like the rehearsals were as taxing as studying for the medical boards while raising three children on your own.

Speaking of Germans, the discussion on poetry was getting *too* lively. I recognized the tone in Regina's voice. She disagreed with something Nigel had said, and now it was about to get weird. Regina had a bachelor's in nothing but was the authority on everything. She would let you dig a hole, talking about something you gave not a shit about, and then pronounce her judgment on it in the same cold tone of voice one might say, "I know he's your best friend, but he raped my sister and murdered her children and I don't understand how you can be friends with him." All conversation would grind to a halt while the person, who somehow found themselves on the wrong side of a discussion of surrealism versus Dada when they thought both were actually kind of crap, would wonder why this woman was so angry about it.

And I was still cutting potatoes! My gravy was as thin as Regina's patience must have been growing, and soon enough I heard the telltale silence that meant that Regina had finally shut Nigel down. Sure enough, she appeared in the kitchen a moment later, complaining about the pompous, chauvinistic old-boy networks of English boarding schools and don't you know they all bugger each other anyway. I was desperate enough that I let her take the knife and finish the potatoes. She was desperate enough to actually do it.

The phone rings again.

"I'm sorry. I just think I need to be home and quiet and read my tarot cards and turn in early. Is that OK?"

Sure it's OK for you to lead me on all day and pretend like you're coming over while I cook with a bad back and where is my brother?!

He finally shows up.

"Happy Thanksgiving, y'all!" (He is not Southern.)

I yell at him, then hug him, then yell at him again.

I notice he has some rather rudimentary stitches on his hand across his knuckles, but I don't say anything knowing I'm not going to get a straight answer anyway.

Time to eat!

We carve the turkey as best as we can, having never done it before. The apartment has an eat-in kitchen; a rarity in the city but perhaps not so uncommon in the part of town where Italian mammas are cooking all day. However, it's still not large enough to fit the seven people I was expecting, nor do I have a table that big. So we sit down to feast in the living room, a small nook between the bedroom and the kitchen, just big enough for a futon and a TV and now the two pushed-together steamer trunks with their candle-wax-stained Indian tapestry tablecloth that we sit cross-legged around. The gravy runs all over the plate but still tastes good, which I suppose is the point. My first attempt at stuffing—I actually bought "stuffing bread" and cut it up and dried it out and cooked it with mushrooms—is somewhat bland but tastes good when soaked in runny gravy.

The "cooking" has worn Regina out and she sits watching everyone eat, shaking her head. She has planted herself next to my brother, since she now refuses to talk to most of the other guests. However, given the cramped size of our dining area, she remains, at most, a foot and a half away from anyone she is trying to avoid. Which perhaps makes it even more obnoxious when she takes out a real honest-to-goodness-for-tobacco-pipe and starts smoking it as that day's affectation, no doubt wondering why no one gets her.

Nigel asks me how I like my school. I think for a moment.

"There's a lot I haven't liked about it. There are many things I hated about it. But looking back on it, I can't say that it's been a bad experience in the end, because it was the things I hated that made me mad, that made me go and seek out other things, and that made me who I am right now, and I'm happy with who I am."

He laughs cynically. "That's a very American answer."

I wonder what that means. I also wonder why lately I am being asked difficult life questions by condescending European men.

Eventually everyone leaves. The dinner portion was a relative success. But that's not the part I care about. Simon is still there. He reclines on my futon, a glass of wine in his hand, and stares up at the ceiling in some manner of existential angst. We talk for a long time. Finally, he gets up to go. It's after two in the morning and as he puts on his coat, he starts talking passionately about Martin Luther King Jr.— no idea how this came up—but he's so strong and passionate and he gets so close to my face, and for a moment I think he's about to kiss me, but he doesn't and I'm excited, and confused, and totally infatuated and God only knows how all of that manifests itself on my face because all of a sudden he stops midsentence and looks concerned.

"What's wrong? Are you OK?"

"Yeah. I'm just confused."

"Why?"

I try to brush it aside. "Nothing."

"No, why?" he insists.

I couldn't help myself. "Because there you go getting all impassioned all over my kitchen, and I feel like kissing you!"

And there it was. Out in the open. All over my kitchen floor. All of the things he could have said next . . . I don't feel that way or I want to kiss you, too, or I have to go. All of the things he could have said . . . this is what he actually says:

"Why?"

"I don't know. I just do. And I feel dumb."

"Well, don't feel dumb."

"But I do. We have a good friendship going here and I don't want to make you feel weird."

"Well, I don't feel weird. I'm just shocked. I'm surprised."

Seriously? He's surprised? We've been hanging out for

the last twelve hours! I cooked a turkey for him! And what about that condom? I make a mental note to look for that paper bag as soon as he's left.

He assures me everything is fine and we hug good-bye making plans to blue ball each other two days from now at the movies or somewhere. As soon as the door closes I look for the paper bag somewhere in the chaos of turkey carcasses and empty Boston Market containers. I find it and look inside. What at first glance looked like a condom, was actually a packet of chamomile tea. I had done all of this in order to have sex with an herbal tea drinker.

But I had had my first taste of a turkey that I had cooked myself, which was in essence, my first taste of freedom. I no longer needed to spend a holiday with my family if I wanted to have a proper meal. Conversely, I no longer had to while away my holiday in a former Eastern Bloc country eating what I hoped was chicken, just because I didn't want to spend it with my family. I could cook a turkey. I could invite the guests of my choosing. I could hold myself to unachievable standards and elaborate ideals that I made up in my head and then feel terribly about myself when I failed to re-create them. I could make myself crazy. I could drink and fight and sob and hate myself through an entire dinner party.

I could do all of that. But I didn't know that then.

Tip

Don't worry if your china lacks a complete setting for eight. You can still set an elegant table and easily distract guests from your mismatched plates with a colorful Indian tapestry that smells like pot, the drama of whether or not your brother is still alive, or your know-it-all friend who has taken six years to finish her theater degree and yet still insists on heatedly debating German poetry with your friend, who is getting his Ph.D. in literature and studied at Oxford.

Recipe
Roasting a Turkey:
So Not the Drama Your Mother Made It Look Like

Ingredients

1 large turkey (18 to 20 pounds)

1 large onion or 2 small onions

1 fist garlic, peeled

Herbs (Just get a bunch of whatever makes you happy. Rosemary. Sage. Thyme. It's all good.)

Salt

Pepper

2 sticks of butter (or olive oil)

2 to 3 cups chicken broth (or turkey broth)

8 tablespoons all-purpose flour (may need more)

OK, if you're like me, you remember your mother cooking turkey for Thanksgiving and making it look like a bigger production than Broadway's *Spider-Man,* and just as fraught with danger. You could get salmonella from the turkey. And if you don't get salmonella from the turkey, you could get it from the stuffing. And if the turkey doesn't kill you, your ungrateful kids will be the death of you.

I'm here to say that cooking a turkey is easy. Yes, it will even be moist. And I'm not some great cook. I have done more wrong things to a turkey than a lonely farmer with a fetish. I have cooked it with the bag of giblets in it. I have cooked turkey in a broken oven so that it took 3 or 4 hours longer than it should have. I have tried the fancy "cook for an hour at 400°F then lower to 325°F" and drank too much and completely forgot to lower the temperature and the turkey cooked so fast I feared it would be tough and dry. And still it has always been edible and even very good. And besides, everyone knows the point of the turkey is to have something to carry gravy into your mouth, and I even figured out how to do that well, eventually.

Here's all you need to do: Take the bag and neck out of your bird. This requires sticking your hand into both the main cavity and the neck cavity. If you only stick your hand into one, you will think you have it all and will miss what's in the other one like I did. Run cold water over your bird inside and out and then pat dry and stick the turkey in your roaster.

You can stuff your bird with stuffing if you want. It will not kill you. Just make sure the internal stuffing temperature is 165°F. I've done that before and it certainly is yummy, but these days I prefer to stuff the cavity of my bird with a quartered onion or two, some garlic cloves, and fistfuls of herbs: sage, rosemary, thyme, whatever you have on hand. Season the outside of the bird with salt and pepper, and then rub a stick of melted butter on it. If cooking for the lactose intolerant, you can use olive oil. I then take 2 or 3 cups of chicken broth (you can use turkey broth if you can find some place that sells it) and pour that over the turkey, too.

You are almost there. See how easy this is already? And we haven't even had to measure anything.

Stick the thermometer in the thickest part of the thigh without touching the bone. Or touch the bone. Honestly, I've done this for years and never been wholly convinced that I have either found the thickest part or that I am not touching bone, and yet my turkeys have cooked and we have eaten them and no one has died. After that you just have to cover the bird, stick it in a 325°F oven, and forget about it while you have a cocktail and make fun of the marching bands in the Thanksgiving Day parade.

Here're the two things I do that I think are really important. Number 1: basting. I baste every hour. You will need one of those sperm-donor-baby-making baster things. The good news is that if it's the day of and you forgot to buy one, they always have them on hand at the local grocery store around Thanksgiving time. Stick the baster in the cavity and pull all of the great juices out and spray all over the top and sides of the bird, like you're filming a porn and the bird is the star. Then put it back in the oven, set the timer for another hour, and have another cocktail.

Number 2: keep the turkey covered. I like to brown the

last 30–60 minutes of cooking, but the rest of the time I keep my bird covered to keep it moist. What's frustrating is that it's very hard to find a roasting pan these days that has a cover. I don't understand why this is. But if you can't find one with a cover, you can use aluminum foil, just be sure to keep it sealed nice and tight on the edges so moisture doesn't escape. But don't cover it too tightly. You want to create a foil tent over the bird so air has room to circulate inside. This is important due to laws of heat and physics that I don't understand, which is why I'm a comedy writer.

Once the turkey reaches the temperature of 165°F you can take it out. Lift it out of the roaster, letting the juices drain off it into the pan, then let it rest on a platter or cutting board. Cover with foil to keep it hot.

And now, gravy!

In a large pot, you're going to make a roux. It's simple, I promise. The rule I go with is 1 tablespoon of butter per tablespoon of flour. For a medium bird I would start with 4 of each. For a larger 18–20 pound bird, I go with 1 full stick of butter and 8 tablespoons of flour. I've also done this with olive oil in place of butter and gotten a wonderful gravy.

Melt the butter first then add the flour. Cook for 1 minute, then pour the pan juices through a strainer into the pot. Stir to mix the roux into the juices thoroughly. The gravy will gradually start to thicken. You can leave it on a low heat and make potatoes or another drink.

If after some time—say 15 minutes or a martini—it's still not as thick as you would like, then you probably just underestimated how much roux you would need. Never fear, you can make some more roux in a smaller saucepan. When that's done, I add a little bit of the gravy that's already made to the small pan, blend in the roux, and then add that mixture back to the main pot. Season with salt and pepper if need be. You've got turkey and gravy and you didn't have to scream that no one ever helps you with anything around here.

Chapter 2
How to Have an Elegant Dinner Party with No Furniture

Now that I knew how to cook a turkey, I wanted to do it all the time. Everyone complained about how difficult it was and yet I could do it and it actually tasted OK. In fact, I was so proud about mastering it, that I actually made up reasons to cook a turkey. A year after my first turkey, I had a Christmas party where I cooked an entire turkey dinner, which was completely ridiculous given that fifty people must have been in and out of my tiny apartment all night. I used every plate I had and I had no dishwasher. That year I actually stuffed the turkey, despite the fact that every hotline and cooking segment told you that you would kill your guests with salmonella. My grandmother had always cooked her turkey with the stuffing in it and not only did we never die, it was delicious. And so was mine that year.

When it actually was Thanksgiving, I was so giddy at the

prospect of showing off the fact that turkeys didn't scare me that I resented invitations to dine elsewhere. That's why I was excited by my first Thanksgiving in LA, because I didn't know anyone who would kill my turkey buzz by being so rude as to invite me to their house.

It was a few years since my first turkey and I had moved to LA just a few months before with my boyfriend. We had both been stand-up comics in Boston, although he was far more successful than I was, having been doing comedy for close to ten years at that point. In fact, it was because of him that I was even in this business. When we met in Boston, he was an established comic and I was a college student who had a bad habit of sleeping with guys I did sketch comedy with. I had done stand-up a few times at a Chinese restaurant to mixed results and quite possibly could have given it up forever, had The Future Boyfriend not offered to get me an audition at the Big Club in Town (not actual name of club). He wasn't even trying to get in my pants; he had a girlfriend! He must think I'm funny, right?

He worked with me on my five-minute audition set and left a message for me the day before I went up—even though he was at the Cape with his girlfriend. He told me to "Just smile and everyone will love you." I listened to that over and over again and heard, "Just smile and everyone will love you. I know I do." And what I remember most is that when I got offstage he was the one waiting for me with a glass of wine and a huge hug to tell me I did great, and not my Actual Boyfriend who was sitting four feet from him and couldn't give a crap what I just did.

Eventually things dissolved with the Actual Boyfriend. Maybe it was because other comics were buying his girlfriend drinks and he couldn't give a crap; maybe it was because in a rage about nothing one day, he sprayed Lysol in my food and threw oranges at me, which technically is attempted murder since I'm allergic to fruit. In any event, things were over between us and I now could focus all of my attention on the secret crush I had always had on Future Boyfriend. He and I were on the phone, still just friends, and he was telling me how he had just been asked to be in the San Francisco Comedy Competition. He would have to go to the Bay Area for at least a week, maybe three if he did well.

"Congratulations," I told him, "I'm really happy for you. That sounds like fun. I'm jealous."

Next came the moment that would change my life forever, in more ways than one.

"You should come," he blurted out. It was totally uncharacteristic for him to say. He's Captain Cautious about everything, always carefully weighing out every option until it's too late to actually proceed with any of them. And yet it was not at all uncharacteristic of me to reply, "Sure!"

I didn't know what I was getting into exactly, I just knew I had an ex-boyfriend throwing fruit at me, a temp job I hated, and a huge crush on the guy on the other end of the phone. Spending an indeterminate amount of time with him three thousand miles away sounded like a great idea.

We ended up being gone for almost a month and two things happened on that trip: first, we fell in love with each other. Then we fell in love with food. When I left Boston, I only drank Chardonnay. I returned not only drinking reds, but ports, too. I now knew the difference between Syrah and Petite Syrah. I could appreciate a big, earthy Cab. I had tried Pinot noir and discovered I hated it! Every moment that my

New Boyfriend wasn't kicking ass in the comedy competition, we spent in Napa or San Francisco or Carmel, eating in fantastic restaurants and tasting great wines. I returned to Boston four weeks later with my standards elevated for both food and men.

Less than a year later we have made the move from Boston to Los Angeles, a far cry from both our idyllic romantic beginnings in wine country and our stable, predictable lives in Boston. We are in LA and as they say in Vietnam, we are in the shit.

The Boyfriend already had reservations about leaving a career that took him several years to build. Some comics do stand-up for years and never make enough money to quit their day job—and sometimes they're even funny. But The Boyfriend was one of the few who was talented and hard working enough that he had no day job. He supported himself solely on stand-up. I was proud of him; it was the realization of a goal he had had since childhood of supporting himself as a performer. I knew he was reluctant to give that up, especially with the uncertainty of how he would fare professionally in LA. Meanwhile, I am shocked to find out that after three whole months, I don't run this town yet. That's not wholly accurate. But whereas in Boston I was shocked when someone said he wanted to help me and he didn't just want to get in my pants, in LA I now find I am shocked when someone says they want to help me and not only do they not want to get in my pants, they don't want to actually help me, either.

My first week in town, The Boyfriend was working a legitimate gig for the weekend at a local club. I got thrown up one night to do a seven-minute guest spot. My first LA spot went so well, the manager of the club came up to me afterward.

"You were fantastic. Really great stuff, really funny. I want you to come back tomorrow night so we can put you on tape. We really need funny women like you at our clubs. I have a meeting with the woman who books them all on Tuesday, she's a really good friend of mine. I'm going to personally hand her your tape and tell her we need to work with you."

I couldn't believe it. Someone was recognizing me for a talent that wasn't how moist I could cook a turkey. I was going to be a regular at this club and I was only in town a week!

Oh, dear, sweet, naïve, Tess. You had no idea. Yes, the manager meant everything he said. And I went back and got myself on tape and it went well. And then he gave the booker the tape. And then nothing happened.

No one cares in LA. Well, no one cares until everyone cares, and then everyone cares. But how do you get everyone caring at once if no one wants to care until someone else does? No idea.

While we were busy trying to figure that riddle out, we started making our way to the various coffee shops and youth hostels and church basements and needle exchanges that passed as comedy shows in Los Angeles. I wasn't afraid of hard work and I certainly didn't expect it to be easy. Boston was a tough comedy town, but if you went up and held your own and made people laugh, you were respected. People would want to book you or at least talk to you. In LA, if you were funny, people either called you a hack or were too threatened to talk to you. Either way it didn't matter because No One cared about you. (See above.)

Sometimes well-meaning friends would give you the

name of someone who ran one of these panic rooms or check-cashing places people new to LA did comedy in, and you would call them but they would barely know your friend and—if you were lucky—tell you that you could do their show only if you brought seven people. This is funny because you don't know seven people, since you just moved here, which is why you are calling this friend-of-a-friend to begin with.

Other times you just had to show up and introduce yourself and watch the wave of disinterest pass over the "booker's" face. In Boston, the booker was someone who had some experience at the club, knew which comedian to book and how often, and which comics would loan him money to gamble with if they had just gotten paid for a set that night. But in LA, bookers were guys who had a microphone and were motivated enough to talk to the coffee shop manager and ask them if they could start a comedy night there. They were only doing this because they wanted to be a comic, so they also didn't like people who were too much funnier than they were, which was usually everybody.

One night soon after I moved there, my friend Bryan and I went to check out a popular coffeehouse that we've heard has a really great show by LA standards, which means that actual working comics with actual TV credits perform at this place where you're lucky if twenty people show up and only fifteen of them are other comics. Bryan and I are college friends from Boston where we did stand-up together, as well, and had moved to LA within a month of each other. Bryan had wisely moved to Los Angeles without a car, so much of our free time is spent together, with me driving us to various open mics held in bus station bathrooms.

Many nights he would take the bus to my place after his

work ended and I would make us turkey tacos with, I am ashamed to say, prepackaged taco spices. It never occurred to me that he should get his own dinner. Where was he going to go anyway, between the bus and my house? I saw no need to make him eat some vile gas-station, egg-salad sandwich just to make a point. I needed to eat and he needed to eat. It seemed logical that we should eat together, share one moment of fun and civility before we went out into the night to get our egos' asses kicked. I think I fed us as a means to gain control in a situation where I had none. I couldn't do anything about the rest of it, but I could do this. That need fulfilled, we would head out to places we had heard about or had seen listed in the *LA Weekly*.

On this one particular night we introduced ourselves to the booker, a monotone-voiced guy who stares at us blankly. I explain that I'm from Boston and that I would love to do his show. I tell him about the club I just performed in and that I can give him a tape of my set.

"Sure . . . ," he slowly drawls in his monotone. "But I mostly just book my friends."

Fair enough.

But I don't give up because I can't. They are all like this and if I was going to say, "Fuck it," I should have just started with the first place months ago. If you're going to quit, quit first thing. Don't quit after you've invested some effort into something, because that's effort you will never get back. To make quitting work for you, you have to quit immediately. And I can't. I don't want to do anything else. I don't even know what I would do. Despite once-promising SAT scores, I have squandered my college years learning to breathe through my diaphragm and have developed no useful skills beyond answering phones and making a decent pot of coffee with substandard coffee grounds. And I can't handle the thought of doing that for the rest of my life! Plus . . . I like this. I like making people laugh. And I think I'm good at it. Stand-up is the culmination of everything I ever wanted to do. Like acting, it's performing, but it's also performing something I've written, that I've created and expresses how I feel.

So I don't quit. I return the next week. And the next four weeks after that. Finally, I am sitting in the back of the coffee shop one night and the booker has decided there needs to be an arm-wrestling competition. I don't know why. I guess once you're already doing a comedy show next to an espresso machine and some really bad art, having an arm-wrestling competition makes perfect sense. He chooses as the first competitor a regular at the café, a man who for lack of a better term, is morbidly obese. This is not an exaggeration done for comedic purposes; there is just no other way to describe him accurately. I could be polite and say he was overweight, but that's just going to give you the image of someone the size of Jonah Hill before he lost all that weight and then this story loses it's impact. Because selected as the challenger was . . . me.

The booker tells me to go up there and wanting to please, I do. I'm also fairly proud of my biceps back then as I was hitting the gym pretty regularly and given the shape my opponent is in, I think I can take him and I do. That's right. The most embarrassing part of the day for him was no longer worrying if he would fit into a chair, it was being beat in arm wrestling by a five foot two inch girl. I humiliated an obese person in front of an audience to make a booker like me.

And that night I was given a spot on an upcoming show. I may have a future in this business.

This was the world we were now living in, but the unusual part of it was that it was surprisingly easy to make friends. Sure, many comics treated you with judgment and suspicion. And many of these "friends" turned out to be borderline personalities who you would soon have enough of, like right around the time they were getting their fifth parking ticket borrowing your car, which is what one of my "LA friends" actually did. But that was OK because it was super easy to make a new friend. In Boston, everyone was so entrenched. They had grown up there or gone to school there and had their friends from so far back they couldn't tell you how they got them. Naturally they were a little suspicious at someone just being nice to them because they wanted a new friend. But no one was from LA. Everyone had just moved there chasing some version of the same ridiculous dream you were and no one knew anybody and it's a town where you need to know everybody. In a town that draws insecure people desperate for the approval of strangers, of course people would get lonely and need to make friends.

Those first few months I met two new friends, both at a comedy show. This means that someone had seen my comedy and still liked me enough to talk to me afterward. The first friend was a fellow comic, a stocky East Coast Italian with a full head of curly black hair named Michael. Michael was not only nice to me, but I thought he was funny, too, and in LA that was a rarer combination than finding someone who had real boobs *and* wasn't on antidepressants.

We met doing a Belly Room show at the Comedy Store, a club that Richard Pryor used to been seen in regularly and that hasn't changed since. The walls were decorated with 1970s style headshots of women with Farrah Fawcett hair and men with mustaches. Today their pictures are probably on a bus stop bench in Florida or Rhode Island, advertising that they can sell you a house. In any event, I had never heard of them, which only underscored my fear of dying anonymous, after getting my real estate license. The green room had a glass coffee table that you would put your drink down on, hoping that the only action it had seen was a lot of lines of coke being cut up and not someone doing a scat scene on top of it.

Michael encouraged me to hang out with him at a local club on Sunday nights where we would try to get the room manager to let us onstage and the bartender gave us comics' prices for beers—seventy-five cents. Not only did he honor the old discount, he considered us comics. I would save up three dollars every week so I could sit down there and try to get onstage. Soon after we started hanging out together there was talk around the clubs that Michael was very, very close friends with an established male comic. I didn't know if it was true or not and I didn't care. I liked Michael.

My other LA friend I met at a place as equally trapped in time as the Comedy Store, but for different reasons. It was a coffee shop decorated to look like an Old West mercantile. I was doing comedy in front of a backdrop of wagon wheels, sacks of sugar, saddles, and antique coffeepots. Sarah came up to me afterward and introduced herself. She wasn't a comic; she had been watching the show and she thought I was funny and wanted to know if I wanted to get together. Not only did I have a new friend, I had a fan!

These are our new friends who we invite to our house for

our first Thanksgiving: Sarah and her animator boyfriend and Michael and his recovering heroin addict girlfriend. We also invite Bryan and another friend of ours from Boston, Rita, who is blind. I haven't changed her name because she is my only blind friend so the jig is sort of up.

With our self-esteem taking a beating on a daily basis—things weren't going much better for The Boyfriend and he actually had experience as someone who got paid to do what he did—it's probably no surprise that we wanted to cook a meal that we could be proud of and left us with a feeling of accomplishment. The Boyfriend had recently learned to make risotto and really wanted to cook some as a side dish. I was hesitant as we were already having potatoes and broccoli; Sarah was bringing muffins, rolls, and carrots; and I was making stuffing. Only this year, I wasn't stuffing the turkey. I was trying a new recipe.

For my day job I was answering phones for a car rental company that accepted cash. Our clientele was people who didn't have a credit card for a variety of reasons, some of which were probably actually legal. But it paid cash and I worked three days a week, which left me time to write and work on stand-up. We got the paper delivered daily, and the highlight of my week was Wednesday, when the food section came out.

I would pore through it each week, taking recipes home with me. Always interested in cooking, we were doing a lot more of it now that we had to save money and The Boyfriend was no longer working in a club six or seven nights a week. Gone are the days when we would grab dinner out before or after his set at the club. Now, we're eating in and shopping at Trader Joe's, and trying to break up the monotony of bean burgers and chicken cutlets. Some days we'd go to Whole Foods and stare at the amazing cuts of meat in the case, dreaming about the day we could buy them.

It's in the food section that I see a recipe from Windows on the World, the restaurant that was in the World Trade Center. It's a cornbread stuffing made with sourdough bread, as well as buttermilk, molasses, and bacon. Intrigued, I decide to try it.

The recipe calls for three cups of homemade or store-bought cornbread, crumbled, so I split the difference and buy a mix that I prepare and then crumble. It's seems a little strange to have something so sweet and cakey in stuffing, but I defer to the sanctity of the recipe.

Thanksgiving day arrives. We sleep in because we're not planning to eat until seven or so. Then, because this is LA, we take an hour-long hike to hopefully combat the effects of the feast we are about to eat. We feel smug wearing shorts and T-shirts when we talk to everyone back East. Eventually we get the bird in the oven, but it's OK because we have plenty of time.

Michael calls and says that they're bringing a pie. The Boyfriend is thrilled because he loves pie and was upset that we weren't going to have any.

I tell Michael, "You just made his day. He's so excited!"

"Thank you, Michael!" The Boyfriend calls from the background.

"Awesome," replies Michael, genuinely pleased with himself.

Our attention turns toward seating. Our 650-square-foot apartment has an open floor plan so that the tiny kitchen looks into the room that is both for eating, watching TV, and writing scripts no one will ever read. Instead of a dining room table, we've opted for an Ikea desk that we both work off of and we eat our dinner sitting at the coffee table (also Ikea) while we watch reruns of *90210*. The TV we watch the aforementioned reruns on sits atop an old coffee table that we rescued from the trash. We decide that if we push the two coffee tables together the eight of us can sit around them Japanese style. Despite the fact that they are two separate heights, we put a paper tablecloth over them and tell ourselves it will be fine.

The Boyfriend leaves to pick up Bryan (no car) and I start to assemble the stuffing, which is gooey and looks sort of disgusting, but I'm hoping it just needs to be baked. When The Boyfriend and Bryan return, I am basting the turkey and growing concerned. The needle on the thermometer is not moving as fast as I would like it to. It's nowhere near the 165°F it needs to be at for me to serve in an hour and that's not even allowing for the time it's going to take to make the gravy. And just like that the buzzer rings, signifying the arrival of the first guest who actually has his own car.

I walk to the elevator to meet them. It's Michael and his girlfriend, Meg. She's tall and thin and very angular with short hair, which probably does nothing to dispel the rumors about her boyfriend.

"We got pie!" Michael says excitedly.

"I know. The Boyfriend is so excited."

"When we heard how excited he was, we got two!" he says enthusiastically.

We arrive back at the apartment and Michael proudly takes out two pink bakery boxes and sets them on the table.

"We got pie," he announces to The Boyfriend.

"When they heard how excited you were, they got two," I add.

"I love pie!" The Boyfriend says, a look of excitement on his face. It's the happiest I've seen him since I made him move out here four months ago.

"Sweet," says, Michael, "because we have two pumpkin pies."

I see the happiest look in four months turn into the disappointed one I now see everyday. The Boyfriend hates pumpkin pie. He loves apple pie, blueberry pie, pecan pie, and cherry pie, but he hates pumpkin pie. Without thinking, we assumed the generic term "pie" meant "pie that he likes" and not "pie that everyone eats on Thanksgiving that he hates." And now he would have to eat it. And eat a lot of it because there were two.

"What can I get everyone to drink?"

Michael says he wants a beer and his sober girlfriend requests a glass of wine.

"Meg is drinking again," Michael says with a shrug like it's the most casual thing in the world that his ex-junkie girlfriend is drinking alcohol.

A bad habit that I have picked up since my younger days, when I would tell everyone to fuck off with abandon, is that I now have the compulsive urge in uncomfortable situations to appear as if I am not judging people's decisions even if I am horrified by them. I need to find a way to emotionally smooth it all out and let them know I'm on their side, even if I'm going to talk about what a crazy bitch they are as soon as they leave, or in a book someday.

"You know," I said, putting on my aforementioned poker

face, "I read that some people don't have a problem with all drugs or alcohol, it's just certain ones that they are addicted to and if they get rid of that, the rest are fine." I didn't read that. I could barely say it. In fact I'm not sure what I actually said is even a sentence.

"She pretty much has a problem with all of them," Michael says with a laugh, like it would amuse him when he found his girlfriend OD'ing in my bathroom later that night.

I turn to The Boyfriend and say under my breath, "Meg is drinking."

He responds with, "I hate pumpkin pie."

I check the turkey again and it's no closer to not killing us, but soon Sarah arrives with her boyfriend, Doug, and then Rita and we all relax with drinks and our new friends and old friends get to know each other. The Boyfriend starts his risotto and not knowing how much to cook for eight people, he opts to make the entire box of Arborio rice. I check on the turkey again and decide that maybe the thermometer is just broken, so I cut into the bird to see if the juices are running clear yet. When they come out pink, I know something is wrong. The turkey has been in since two and it's after eight. Our eighteen-pound turkey (I like a lot of leftovers, so?) should have taken four and a half, maybe five hours, tops to roast. It's been more than six and it's not even near done. The juices don't lie.

I look at The Boyfriend, "I don't know what to do. I think the oven is broken."

The Boyfriend is stirring a gigantic pot of rice on the stove. He puts in an entire container of parmesan Reggiano. Well, at least if this turkey never cooks, we will have plenty of risotto.

I now have to go explain to our six guests, four of whom I barely know and one who has just fallen off the wagon, that dinner is still not ready.

"I'm really sorry. I don't know what the problem is. It should be done by now. I've done this a bunch of times before and never had a problem like this."

Now the turkey—the thing that I was so proud I could cook—has failed me. My stuffing has come out of the oven looking no more edible than it did when it went in. I start peeling potatoes for something to do. I look to Bryan, but he's busy looking at Meg and Michael with the same look of confusion: Meg because she looks a little strung out but he still finds her attractive; Michael because he's heard the rumors, too.

I check the turkey again. It's getting near nine o'clock. And yet despite my panic, everyone is totally cool. Everyone is getting along. Bryan is enjoying hearing about the cartoon Doug is working on. Rita is letting Meg bum cigarettes off of her. The table is uneven, the turkey isn't done, and the stuffing looks like someone vomited up a Missoni sweater, but still I think the night feels like a success.

Finally, the turkey is ready. I rush through the gravy—it was never going to thicken anyway—and soon it is time to eat. We serve ourselves buffet style before bringing our plates back to the table. Meg stands next to me as I try to explain the stuffing.

"It's molasses, and sourdough, and cornbread with buttermilk. . . . I just thought it sounded really interesting," I finish doubtfully.

Meg inadvertently comes to my rescue, "You know how

some flavors seem like they wouldn't go together, but when you put them together they actually do?"

People are loading up on carrots and potatoes and rolls, but no one is touching the risotto, despite the fact that it's quite good. I feel bad for The Boyfriend; he wanted to impress people with something he could do well, too.

"Save room for pie," Michael announces.

We still had to get through dessert. The moment of truth was coming for The Boyfriend who knew he could not *not* eat pie after making such a big deal about it. I watched The Boyfriend choke down two pieces of pumpkin pie so as to not hurt Michael's feelings. He put lots of coffee ice cream on it to make it go down easier. I didn't ask Michael if that's what he does with the male comic.

Eventually everyone started to leave. Sarah and Doug gave Rita a ride home, since it was on the way, and Doug offered to send Bryan a book of his cartoons. Michael and Meg leave without us even having to call the paramedics or Dr. Drew. Bryan stayed behind for a drink before The Boyfriend and I drove him home. The three of us sat out on the balcony, stuffed, thankful for the break from daily LA life.

"You know how some flavors seem like they wouldn't go together, but when you put them together they actually do?"

The stuffing was horrible. I think I later burned the recipe. But the night was perfect.

We would have many Thanksgivings after that, but never with those same people. But I always, every year, make The Boyfriend an apple pie. Just in case.

Tip

We're all happy when we learn to make new things. How exciting! However, no one wants to try your new things on Thanksgiving. On Thanksgiving, you're like Styx in concert: stick to the hits. People want turkey, stuffing, potatoes, and gravy. I think it's great that you can cook risotto now, but if you cook it on Thanksgiving you're going to end up dumping a large pot of Arborio rice and parmesan cheese in the garbage, which is going to make your girlfriend cry while she says, "I told you so," through tears.

Recipe
Apple Pie: Because Store-Bought Is for People Who Don't Love Their Boyfriends

Ingredients

2 cups flour

11 tablespoons butter

⅓ cup cold water

4 or 5 large apples

2 pints blueberries

½ cup sugar

1 to 2 tablespoons flour

1 egg

Cinnamon or nutmeg to taste

After the Great Pumpkin Pie debacle, I made it my business to learn how to cook pie for The Boyfriend. This provided some interesting challenges. As I cannot eat fruit I was unable to test each endeavor, which left me completely unable to perfect my recipe by the usual methods. I had to rely on The Boyfriend's feedback and I learned that when it comes to pie, men pretty much feel the same way they do about a naked woman. Any one is great. They're totally grateful the first time you give them pie, and they don't take it for granted that they will ever see one again.

Pies really aren't that hard. You make a crust, lay it out in the pan, stick your fruit on top of it, and then put the crust on top. That's it. It's more complicated to make a sandwich. Pies aren't hard; they're tricky.

Take the crust. It's 2 cups of flour, 11 tablespoons of butter, and ⅓ cup of cold water, although I'm sure I've used room temp and it was all fine. (See "naked woman" above.) Nowadays I have a food processor, a handy invention that allows me to stick all of the ingredients into it and hit ON until I have a nice little dough ball, or at least something that I can make into one. However I used to not have a food processor and had to mix the ingredients myself. See? Tricky.

Some people have pastry cutters and I suppose have good luck with them. I haven't used one since seventh grade Home Ec. Instead, I would employ a knife and fork. After letting the butter soften, I would place the flour in a bowl. I would then make a well in the middle of the bowl, cut the butter up into small pieces, and slowly slice at the butter with my knife and fork, mixing it in with the flour as I went around the bowl, periodically pouring a small amount of water into the well in the middle, stirring that in as well. You want to get all of your ingredients mixed, but it's a very dry proposition and takes some patience, of which I have none, by the way. I used to just cheat by adding more water to make my dough, but I learned somewhere along the way that this led to a very heavy, unflaky crust. I recommend getting it somewhat mixed, then spilling it all out onto the counter where you can knead it together the rest of the way. I also recommend investing in a food processor if you think you're going to be making a lot of pie.

Once it's smooth and in a ball, you want to split it into two pieces. Roll out one so that it's big enough to cover the bottom and sides of your pie pan. You want it to hang over a little so you can sew the pie up at the end. You can use a rolling pin, although in a pinch I have also used a large, 20-ounce bottle of microbrew beer. Take a swig of the beer, you're halfway done.

Next comes the filling. Pick your fruit. You can use frozen, but don't do what I did and skip the part where it says to let the fruit defrost first, and just throw it into the pie frozen thinking, "What the hell could it possibly matter?" The fruit will defrost as it cooks, yielding extra water and giving you a runny pie. Look, I would tell you if you could skip something, you know I would. If you're really impatient, get fresh fruit. It will taste better anyway. Generally speaking you need 4 or 5 large apples and a couple of pints of blueberries. Eyeball it. If you have extra fruit, you can always stick it in a ramekin and bake it in the oven and serve with whip cream or ice cream or just the rest of that beer.

If you go with apples, you have to peel them. I'm not going to lie to you: this is a pain in the ass. Blueberries are much easier. I suggest you find a motivated boyfriend who wants apple pie badly enough to help you, like I do. Also get a decent peeler and not the rusty one your mom has been using since the '80s. That will help, too. Once you have the apples peeled, you need to cut them into pieces, cutting around the core in the center. Or you could buy a Crate and Barrel apple corer for about ten bucks that cores them while slicing them into slices. This is a great gadget, although you still may want to slice at least some of the apples into smaller pieces still.

So you take your fruit, put it into Tupperware with ½ cup of sugar, 1–2 tablespoons of flour, and I like to add some cinnamon and nutmeg, and shake until the fruit is evenly coated with all of it. Then you pour it into the pan. You roll out the remaining piece of dough to place over the top. The pie will need a vent, so I like to take a small cookie cutter and cut out a piece of dough. After I've put the top piece on, I like to put the part I cut out on top, like a decoration. Join the edges of the top and bottom pieces, pinching them together, you know like they do with pies. You can beat an egg to brush the top of the crust that will make it shiny and also help the decorative piece stick.

One time recently I was making dough and it was so dry I couldn't roll the top piece out without it just cracking. I don't know if the butter was too cold or if I didn't use enough water, but one thing was certain: I was never getting this top part in one piece across the pie. I was stuck. It was about eight in the morning and I had been at this since at least 7:30, having had the bright idea that I would get it out of the way early so that I could relax in the afternoon. I was unshowered, uncaffeinated, and covered in flour. I hadn't eaten breakfast yet and I couldn't bear the thought that I would have to make a fresh batch of dough, even with my food processor.

It dawned on me that I could do a lattice pie, you know one where strips of dough crisscross the pie top? Only I didn't have a fancy, wheely pastry thing to cut the dough into strips with. (In retrospect I probably could have used a pizza cutter, but again, it was eight in the morning and I hadn't had coffee.) Then I got a great idea. I would use a cookie cutter to cut out stars, it was Christmas after all, and then layer the stars over the top of the pie using an egg wash to help them stick to each other, leaving gaps in between some of them to serve as vents. I was skeptical it would work, but an hour later it came out of the oven looking beautiful.

Some things are just too beautiful for this world. This pie was one of them. The following night at dinner, as the guests arrived, each one passed where the pie was on display, remarking about how gorgeous it was and how they couldn't wait to eat it. When it was time for dessert I walked into the dining room triumphantly carrying a cake stand in each hand, one for the flourless chocolate cake, the other with the pie on top. And that's when it happened. The pie pan started to slide across the cake stand it was on. Back and forth until it became airborne, flipping over and landing star side down on the floor. THUD.

I didn't lose my cool. I laughed about it and so did everyone else. And then one of my male guests said completely in earnest, "I don't know about the rest of you, but I'm still having some of that pie."

See? Naked woman.

He was as good as his word and so were many other guests. People still ate the pie that night and they thought it was great. So relax. You're not taking a tumor out of a child's brain. You're cooking. You are bound to not do things perfectly. But no matter what you mess up, people will still want to eat your food and even find it delicious.

Chapter 3
How to Enjoy a Good Meal with Friends

If you've never moved to LA to break into the entertainment business, treat yourself and don't. It's awful. If I had to do it all again...I would have done it sooner. Because no amount of time that you have seems like it's enough. The problem with coming here to "make it" as they say in old movies, is that you never know *if* you're going to make it until you do. Conversely, you also never know that you won't "make it," either. That's what keeps people here forever and ever doing insufferable plays and commercial auditions.

I don't like to use the word "struggle" to describe our first year. "Struggle" makes it sound like there's something you're actually doing and many times in LA, you're not doing anything but waiting. People struggle when they lift something heavy, or run in the heat. When you're waiting for someone to call you back the only thing you're really struggling with is whether or not this is some alternate reality that Sartre wrote about. I don't know the word to describe years of working hard to get yourself and your ideas out there and then not hearing anything. Anything. And realizing one year and then another has passed and absolutely nothing has changed. You're still waiting to see how this ends.

Fuck it was tough.

That's the only thing I really know to say about it. For starters, as every East Coast transplant is fond of chanting, LA is no *Fill in Name of East Coast City*. The buildings here are new and ugly. And when I walked around my neighborhood in sneakers and sweats, people thought I was a hooker, because apparently even the hookers underdress here. And one parking ticket would throw off my budget for the whole month and make me cry. You would meet someone who thought you were talented and then they would never call you back. Someone would give your script to an agent and the agent would never call you back. Someone would tell you to call them about a job and they would never call you back. And everywhere around you, people would tell you about all of the big things they had going on and it made you feel like you were some talentless nobody because you had nothing going on. It took me years to learn two things. Number 1: people were mostly lying. Number 2: when you finally had the same things happening to you that they used to brag about, you realized that this thing you were once jealous of wasn't going to make you rich and probably wasn't going to happen, anyway.

I'd like to say that, "Through it all we had each other," but that's not always true. The frustration and uncertainty could be unbearable for one person, and sharing it among two people doesn't lighten the load. It makes it heavier. They have their own disappointment and fear and can't answer your questions and tell you it will all be OK. They don't believe it about themselves, how can they say it about you? And when they can't predict the future for you, you hate them a little for it. But most of all, you can't bear the deep sadness you feel when you see someone you love so frustrated and disappointed and there is nothing you can do to help.

This is what our first year is like, once the wonder of seeing the sun every day of the year wears off. You don't just wait to have calls returned; you wait everywhere in LA. In traffic. At the grocery store. In the post office. I didn't understand why popping in to pick up a bottle of wine and a pint of ice cream turned into a forty-five minute ordeal, no matter what time of the day or night you went. Finally, The Boyfriend figured it out: no one here has a job. No one has a schedule. No one ever has to be anywhere. They go to the store at eleven in the morning, at four in the afternoon, at twelve o'clock at night. The post office, too, resembled a bread line in Russia. I had availed myself of the post office many times in other parts of the country, and even the world, and had never seen anything like it. Soon enough I realized that I was standing behind a guy with seven screenplays he was sending to agents, and he was next to a girl with a hundred headshots. Then I got it. The post office didn't work because everyone was clogging it up with failure. You didn't just struggle in your career in LA; it was a struggle just to get through the day.

AUTHOR'S NOTE: Not like people struggle through the day to escape warlords or find clean drinking water. "Struggle" like self-absorbed people struggle for comedic purposes.

We had been there a little over a year when The Boyfriend's old roommate called to tell us he'd be performing in Vegas Labor Day weekend. Kevin Knox was a legend in the Boston comedy scene, but despite this I walked out of his show the first two times I saw him perform. I had not yet met The Boyfriend and was still the pretentious liberal arts student who took herself way too seriously. I was watching a local comedy show because I had a friend performing and eventually it was time for the headliner. Kevin Knox took the stage in shorts, sneakers, a nylon track jacket zipped halfway up with no shirt under it, his mullet flapping in the breeze. You heard me. Mullet.

"Who the fuck is this guy?" I thought.

Kevin started tearing up the room, making everyone laugh hysterically, everyone but me. I turned to my friend. "I think it's sexist when men portray women as having these cartoonishly high voices," I said as I put money for my beer on the table and took off.

A few weeks pass. I'm with another friend at another comedy club. And once again, when the host announces the headliner . . .

"Oh, Jesus. Not this guy again! What the fuck! He's everywhere!"

And I took off again.

Imagine then my surprise, the first time I go to The Boyfriend's apartment and I scan for the buzzer with his name on it, only to see right beside his name: K. Knox.

You've got to be kidding me. He *is* everywhere!

But The Boyfriend is so enlightened, so smart. He went to Bowdoin. How could he live with this mulleted misogynist?

This "mulleted misogynist" quickly became one of my favorite people in the world. I don't say that hyperbolically; of all the people I have ever known, he was one of my favorites. It was impossible to be sad around Knoxie. He was too much fun to be with. Everyplace he went, he walked in—over six feet tall with a personality just as big—greeting everyone with whom he came into contact. If he had been there more than once, he knew everyone by name. And most importantly, Knox was the only person I ever saw who could make The Boyfriend relax. The Boyfriend was perpetually stressed, even before we moved to Los Angeles and I put his entire financial future in jeopardy. Now LA only intensified his usual fear that the worst was going to happen and he'd die with no money for retirement. It was a constant concern of his despite it being decades away. One of the many things that made me fall in love with him was his maturity and sense of responsibility, but I worried that he was too focused on the end of our lives, as if the time in between didn't matter. But Kevin had a way of making it OK that we were just hanging out, not doing anything that in any way could benefit our careers or contribute to our retirement. Kevin was coming to Vegas, and damn it we were going to meet him there.

Despite living in such close proximity to it for over a year, I had had no desire to go to Las Vegas. I didn't gamble; I didn't do buffets; I didn't want to get married. It seemed to me the Temple to All Things Tacky, the physical manifestation of everything wrong with the country and I had no desire to see. But I had a huge desire to see Knox.

We drove out the Monday of Labor Day weekend, laughing about all the suckers stuck in the desert traffic going in the opposite direction. This was a bonus of having no job; we could go away after the holiday weekend was over.

On the drive out I am given instructions. Knox isn't the only one in Vegas that week; he's being joined by two of his best friends, Frank and Joe. Frank was the general manager at the club back in Boston where The Boyfriend and I met. He was a barrel-chested, red-faced Boston Irishman, with a large heart and a large appetite for both food and life. But Frank was more reserved than Knox. Whereas Knoxie walked into a room and greeted everyone, Frank was already sitting there and like a Don, would wait for you to come to him. Joe tended bar at the restaurant we all hung out at before, after, and during the comedy shows at the club across the street. The only one of the threesome who was married, he shared Frank's passion for food and also looked out for him if he sat at a blackjack table a little too long. A few times a year, Knox would do stand-up in Vegas for a week, and Frank and Joe would fly out. The threesome would spend the week golfing and hanging out by the pool. When Knox went off to do his shows, Frank and Joe would check out one of the new restaurants in town and then they would meet up for drinking and gambling. It was the perfect guys' week. And I was infiltrating it.

I don't know if I was the first girl allowed on this trip or just the first one who actually asked to go. But as such, my behavior would determine whether or not I was the last. I was like Sandra Day O'Connor. I knew everyone would be watching what I did, judging to see if I fit in. I wasn't to complain about the quality of the alcohol and I was to keep up with the guys.

I accept my assignment and in just over four hours we arrive at the Tropicana where Knox is performing. We have just enough time to drop our stuff in his room before his first show of the night. This time I don't walk out. Instead, I know all of his bits by heart and The Boyfriend and I recite them to each other like we're singing along to our favorite songs at a U2 concert. Now, we are the ones doing the high-pitched female voices and laughing at the silliness of it all.

When Kevin is finished, we head over to meet Frank and Joe at the Big Apple bar inside New York, New York across the street. I am shocked when we walk right out of the Trop still holding our drinks in our hands.

"We can do this?"

"Sure. It's Vegas, Baby!" is Kevin's boisterous reply.

I wonder if there's some exchange of glassware done between the hotels at the end of the week. They really don't care if I leave the Trop's rocks glass at the MGM? I get annoyed every time a glass breaks and I have to replace it or risk having an uneven set.

We find Frank and Joe and a round of drinks gets ordered. We all start to catch up and before long we are on our way to another bar where another round gets ordered. I am not even finished with the first round, but I don't say no. Instead, when no one is looking, I leave the first drink somewhere else. I am drinking beer tonight, instead of wine, knowing that most bars will have wine not up to even my meager standards at the time, plus I'm under strict orders to not complain about the alcohol. Despite the time of night, it's still incredibly hot out and as we walk around from casino to casino my beers are getting so warm I don't mind dumping them at the next destination. I will do this trip many times in the future; I will ask for better alcohol and I will say "No" to a round when I've had enough. But first I had to earn that right on this trip.

We drink and watch Frank play blackjack. We drink and watch bad lounge acts. We go back to the Trop to meet Knox after his second show and stay for another round in the lounge. The singer is a perky, forty-something woman with a short, curly bob. She wears a red, sequined onesie that seems like overkill for the eleven people sitting in front of her, five of whom are us. After a few songs Frank starts grumbling, "She hasn't played Gloria Estefan yet. Usually she plays that Gloria Estefan 'Everlasting Love' song." On my way to the bathroom where I dump Bud number four, I ask her to play the song for Frank. And when I come back she is dedicating it to "Frankie." He looks annoyed but at the end he says, "She does a good job."

It is early in the morning when we go back to Knoxie's room. Rather than sleep in a king all week, he has gotten a room with two doubles so that we wouldn't have to get a hotel. The three of us watch TV like we used to when they were roommates as we fall asleep.

We wake up late the next day and after breakfast we meet Frank and Joe at the Mandalay Bay where they are staying and spend the afternoon at the pool. Up until this point, I was not really much of a: a) pool person, b) Vegas person, or a c) afternoon drinker.

And yet there I was, lounging at a Vegas pool, reading as drinks are brought to me. When we got too hot, we all jumped in the wave pool and swam and then we got out and ordered another round of drinks. Joe and Frank are charging them to their room. We feel guilty but relieved when we offer to pay and they wave us off. "Later," they say.

It was a relaxing afternoon, possibly the first one we had had in a year. It was certainly the first time since we had moved that we were able to have fun without thinking about what we should have been doing, as if this afternoon spent doing nothing would somehow cost us an opportunity down the road. We were able to have conversations that weren't framed in the context of our most recent rejection. We were no longer two people struggling to be something in LA and fearing this was it and nothing would ever happen to us. We were a couple, hanging out with good friends from Boston who liked us no matter what we did.

Soon talk turns to where Joe and Frank are going to eat that night. They decide on Emeril's New Orleans Fish House at the MGM and go to make a reservation. "You guys are coming, right?" Frank says. It's more of a statement than a question.

"Awww... man, we'd love to but we can't," The Boyfriend tries to say casually. We don't want to draw attention to the fact that we are broke. We don't want to make anyone uncomfortable, like we're looking for sympathy for our bad decisions.

"It's OK," Frank replied. "You're with me."

"Really, Frank, we just don't have the money right now for something like—"

"You're with me," he insisted.

That night, I got my first lesson in how to do a dinner, Frank and Joe style. We met before dinner at the restaurant bar and had a cocktail. For me that night it was a rum and ginger ale, which while not sophisticated, incorporated the one mixer and one liquor that I actually liked at the time. Then we sat down to eat. A bottle of white was ordered while we looked over the menu. Not paying for myself, I didn't want to order an appetizer, but Frank ordered several for the whole table. A bottle of red was ordered.

Now we got down to the business of entrées. I had a lot of questions. I always have a lot of questions. I'm allergic to a lot of food that often finds its way into dishes, even if it's not listed on the menu. For example, I can't eat fruit. Any fruit. I know, it's weird. No one understands how it is I manage to live except doctors who think fruit is highly overrated, it turns out. I try to tell waiters I can't have fruit first thing and often what I hear back is something like this:

"Not a problem. There's no fruit in the grilled shrimp. It's just grilled with some salt and pepper and finished with a little lime juice."

"Lime is a fruit."

"Oh, right. . . ."

Other times I order something like polenta with mushrooms, an earthy dish that shouldn't have citrus anywhere near it, and yet someone comes back and tells me that the polenta has lemon in it. Ewww. Just because I can't eat fruit, doesn't mean I can't appreciate what it would taste like if you added it to something. Just because I don't eat fruit doesn't mean I won't realize when you're misguidedly trying to fancy up your grits with some lemon juice.

Also, I can't have certain vegetables, and this is where things get complicated. So I talk to the waiter. A lot. We become good friends. They usually have to ask the chef some questions and then report back to me. It's a process. It's like dining with Meg Ryan in *When Harry Met Sally* minus the faking the orgasm part.

So the waiter and I were getting acquainted over the list of entrées and he disappears to talk to the chef. When he comes back, he asks me to list the things I'm not allergic to and says the chef is going to prepare me something special. I can't believe it. At best, I am usually treated as the customer who comes in the door five minutes before closing on Christmas Eve. Sometimes, I am treated as if I shouldn't even attempt to eat in a restaurant. One time, a waiter condescendingly suggested to me that I treat my allergies holistically, because that's how he cured his food allergies. Oh, is that what you recommend? I'm pretty sure you're not a doctor, and frankly I'm not even really sure you're a waiter. But making me something special? This night was magic.

There are oysters and clam chowder and grilled shrimp (without lime juice.) We catch up on the gossip about all of the comedians back home. We hear stories of a club booker with the bad coke problem and the even worse gambling problem and how he put four of the girls at his club in jeopardy by trying to hide from the thugs he owed money to when they were working. Joe and I spend some time discussing what books we're reading. The entrées come and the red wine is poured. I had gotten salmon, blackened, and they served it on a bed of mushrooms, potatoes, and onions. It was literally everything I could eat. Salmon was a luxury then. But it was one of my favorite foods. The Boyfriend would sometimes perform at a club in Hermosa Beach. It was at least an hour away in traffic, but they let you and your guest eat for free. I would always opt to make the trek with him and spend the night down there, because they had salmon on the menu.

We were stuffed and there was still more to come. Dessert was ordered and with dessert coffee and liqueurs. Frank always had an espresso and a sambuca. Giddy from the variety of délicious tastes and the excitement of the ritual, I ordered a cappuccino and a Baileys. Finally there is nothing left to eat or drink. Sated, we go out into the Vegas night to meet Knoxie.

We would make this trip many times over the years. Knoxie always offered us his room to save us money. Our next trip out he went out of his way to pay for our dinner. Eventually, we were able to save the money to pay for our own dinner the next time and then the time after that we got our own room at the Trop. The last time we were all together there we stayed at the Paris. I had been working at *The Soup* for almost a year.

That last trip Kevin had already been diagnosed with cancer nine months previous. He had had skin cancer before but it was in remission. This time it had moved to his lymph system. It was September in Vegas again and still hot. Knox pulled up to meet us at the Paris; the mullet was shaved but he still had a big grin on his face. He was driving a convertible and not wearing a shirt. "What are you doing driving a convertible, bald and with no shirt on? Do you not know you have cancer?" I half teased and half reprimanded him.

For the first few years in LA, we had gone back to Boston at least twice a year. We always stayed with Knoxie. We never really had the money to travel, but we always did it anyway. Knoxie would sweet-talk the people at his gym into letting us work out for free. We slept on his pull-out couch, even though it was the most uncomfortable bed we were offered. He called us "the kids," and referred to us as "being home from college to visit the old man." Whenever we saw him—in Vegas or Boston—I would always try to bring him cookies. Once for dinner I had seen him devour two slices of pizza, a lemon square, a large turkey sub, and a salad. And then for dessert he had one and a half packages of Nutter Butters. Not snack size. Actual packages. It was a sight to behold and the memory always makes me laugh. He was in shape, but he lived large. He was so happy that night eating all of those cookies. I always tried to bring him some because the thought of making him that happy made me happy. I wanted to try and make him as happy as he had always made us.

When he got cancer, he traded his big appetite for a raw diet. The man who once inhaled two entire packages of cookies rarely complained about the fruit and nuts he was now restricted to. Instead, he would still go to dinner with us in Vegas, opting to order just a salad that he would eat with a specially prepared dressing he carried with him. The meal was more important than the food. The important thing was that we were all together.

The irony is that when we finally had the money to go back to Boston, we never went. We were too busy. By that last Vegas trip we were both working steadily, which was great, but steady work meant we could no longer travel the day after holiday weekends anymore. It had been three years since we had been back when we got the call that he didn't have long. Kevin had an inoperable mass on his lung that was pressing on his heart. It's the day before my birthday and I'm on the treadmill in the garage, thinking of the Vegas trips and all of our good times in Boston. And I am crying and running when the realization hits me that I wouldn't be here on a treadmill, in my garage, in my backyard, looking at our pool if it weren't for Kevin Knox. We couldn't have stuck it out through all of that crap to get to the good stuff if it wasn't for his positive influence. I called him up and left a message, "Everything we have we owe to you."

We went back to see him the following weekend. Six weeks later he was gone. And eight months after that, so was Frank.

These two men did so much for us. In the desert, they managed to create an oasis for us: an oasis from LA, from the grind and uncertainty and fear and fights and post office. But I learned a lot from them, too. I learned to keep your friends close because life is short. And to do things when you don't have the money, because someday you may run out of time, for good. To take time out to be a person and not a career path. I learned to try to be generous to my friends in their honor. But most of all, I learned the basic joy of sharing a delicious meal and fantastic wine with friends. Frank instilled that in me. And every time I raise a glass around my table and look at the friends surrounding me, I drink to them.

Tip

Remember that a meal—whether cooking for friends or going out to a restaurant—is about celebrating being together. Always keep in mind that what you will remember years later is not what went wrong, but that you were together.

Recipe
Knoxie's Cookies:
For Someone Whose Appetite
for Food Is as Big as Their
Appetite for Life

Ingredients

2 sticks butter
¾ cup white sugar
¾ cup brown sugar
1 teaspoon vanilla
2 eggs
¼ teaspoon salt
1 teaspoon baking soda
2 to 2½ cups flour
1 package chocolate chips
Extras (see recipe)

Cookies are the quiche of the dessert world. Once you master the basic recipe, you can take all sorts of liberties, customizing it to fit your own preferences and discovering all sorts of new flavor combinations. That's how I used to do it when I sent cookies to Knoxie; I used to love the image of him opening a box and finding more cookies than he knew what to do with inside.

Again, this is the type of endeavor that is easier if you have something like a KitchenAid, and who wouldn't want one? They come in all sorts of colors and once you spend nearly three hundred dollars on one, your boyfriend can't very well tell you to go out and get a new one, even if he feels having a lavender one in the kitchen emasculates him slightly. Men are silly. Do we look at the size of the TV hanging on the wall and say that it makes us feel as if we're having a hysterectomy? No. We realize it makes them happy and keeps them quietly anesthetized in the glow of its thirty-nine inches.

However, if you don't have a KitchenAid (yet) I recommend an electric hand mixer. I've never made cookies with a wooden spoon and my own sheer determination, although more power to you if you have. Your arms probably look prettier in a tank top than mine.

So here's the recipe used since time immemorial: you cream 2 sticks of butter, add ¾ cup of white sugar, ¾ cup of brown sugar, 1 teaspoon of vanilla, and 2 eggs. Once that is good and mixed, you add your dry ingredients: ¼ teaspoon salt, and 1 teaspoon baking soda, and 2–2½ cups of flour. (Sometimes the dough gets to the right consistency with less flour and sometimes it needs more, for reasons that are probably scientifically explainable, like I'm not very particular about measuring. Be your own judge.) You then add your chocolate chips.

However, get creative. You can also add chopped-up nuts. Or chopped-up pretzels, for a wonderful salty/sweet thing. Speaking of salty, sometimes I make regular chocolate chips and then just sprinkle sea salt on top right before they go into the oven. You can add less flour and a cup or so of quick cooking oats to the mix and have oatmeal cookies. I like to also add butterscotch chips and a teaspoon of cinnamon when I do this. You don't have to use two kinds of sugar. You can use all white for a lighter cookie, or all brown for a more molasses taste. Add cocoa to the flour mixture for a choco- late cookie. Add 1 teaspoon or 2 of instant espresso pow- der to that for a mocha cookie! Crush candy canes and add them to your chocolate cookie for the holidays! Be on the lookout for different things in the baking aisle. I once found cappuccino chips. Another time, I found little chocolate mint chips. Buy them when you see them and experiment with them later. It's not like they'll go bad. Trust me. I just made butterscotch oatmeal cookies with butterscotch chips that expired a year and a half ago. What's to go bad? Everything in them is already artificial. Instead we said that our chips were finely aged and the cookies were delicious and no one died.

Once you've finalized the details on your cookie canvas, drop them by the spoonful onto a cookie sheet. I prefer to lay parchment paper down on mine first because they come up easily with no cooking spray or butter and it also minimizes clean up. (READ: I just throw the paper away and put the pans back in the cabinet.) Cook them in a 375°F oven for about 10 minutes, adjusting the time according to how dark and crisp you like your cookie.

Chapter 4
How to Throw an Impromptu Dinner Party for 7 at 1 a.m.

We've been in LA for almost three years now. We still live in the same apartment; we still don't have jobs; we're still waiting for phone calls to be returned. But we have friends. Not crazy friends who are really having sex with guys but bring their junkie girlfriends to your house for Thanksgiving. What looks like actual, lifelong friends.

Heather and I met at a mutual friend's wedding, in the buffet line. I was asking the chef my requisite number of ridiculous questions, as per usual, and I noticed she was doing the same.

"Do you have food allergies?" I asked, excited to find one like me.

"Oh, yeah. You, too?"

We sat next to each other and talked all night. I liked that she was very straightforward and blunt and was particularly grateful for it at the end of the night. We had both had a lot to drink; the kind of "a lot to drink" where you're laughing with friends one minute and then a Shania Twain song comes on and you burst into tears and hope someone cuts you off. We were standing on the edge of the dance floor when one comic grabbed his girlfriend and pulled her onto his lap. He then dipped her backward so her skirt comes up and I see, up and down her thighs, huge bruises. It was strange. I didn't for a second think they were inflicted by her date, which somehow made it even stranger. I don't remember if I was pre– or post–Shania Twain melt-down when it happened, but nonetheless, I was in a state where I wasn't sure if it was actually happening. Surely, I was hallucinating this. Then I turned to Heather. She was staring at the bruised thighs, too.

"Do you see—" I started to ask.

"The bruised thighs?" she interrupted. "Yeah, that's weird."

We left that night as friends, always referring to the girl as "Bruisey Thighs" every time one of us saw her.

I also had enough friends at this point, that they would rope me into foolish things like trying to run my own night of comedy at a local coffee shop. Not enough friends to actually come to said night but just enough to suggest I do it with them.

This is the conundrum of doing comedy in LA. You need to get stage time in order to develop. It's easier to get stage time if you do your own show. Not only can you book your-self, but then everyone who wants to be on your show in turn books you on theirs. However, it's a colossal pain in the ass to get people to actually attend a comedy show in a cof-fee shop. I'd get less disinterested stares if I were asking for money for the Republican party. Sure, every once in a while you would get lucky and you'd get thirty people. But when you're telling jokes in front of four people eventually you have to wonder if this is really helping you develop into anything besides an alcoholic.

And that's not even dealing with the perpetual disappointment of the people who own the establishment. They expect you to fill the place with zero budget for promotion, as if they're going to get rich anyway by selling twenty cups of coffee as opposed to seven. It's not my fault your dream was to own a coffee shop instead of a steak house.

So here I was producing this comedy show, which was and is my least favorite thing to do in the world, because it's like having a birthday party every week that no one shows up for. Fortunately this "coffee shop" served wine. It was shitty coffee-shop wine, but it helped me get through the nine acts I was bringing to the stage (two more than actual audience members) and the conversation I eventually had with the proprietor afterward.

"I don't think this is working out," he says.

Really?! Because I think this is going great!

No shit, it wasn't working out. Add that to the list of other things not working out in my life right now. Earlier that year I had gotten really close to getting into a prominent comedy festival. I didn't expect it. But the night I auditioned I had a really great set. Everything had just come together. Before I went onstage I said to myself, "Remember this." And I did. I was totally in the moment. I knew it went great.

Afterward, a woman who was a manager, but wasn't *my* manager, even though she sometimes called me with opportunities and always bought me drinks on her expense account, said, "I think I'm going to need to buy a winter coat." (The festival was some place cold.) The next day Not My Manager called and said, "They want to bring you back for an executive callback!" She told me what to change, what to work on. I went to the callbacks and they went great!

Then I waited.

I waited a few weeks and then they turned into months. Finally I heard. I didn't get in. They said they wanted to see me develop for an extra year.

And that's when people started congratulating me.

Every club I went to, people said, "I heard you got in. Congratulations!"

Not My Manager called back to double-check. Nope. Still hadn't gotten in. Turns out there was a black comedienne, also named "Tess." She was going.

So now when I walked in and heard, "Congratulations!" I immediately said, "No, that was the other Tess. There's a black one and a white one. She got in."

And that's when I heard, "Are you sure? I don't think so. I definitely heard 'Tess Rafferty.'"

In addition to the constant reminder of my failure, I was now being confused with her in other areas, too. One night a comic walked into the Improv and yelled at me. "Where were you? You were supposed to open for me in Brea last night!"

And then I had to explain to him that I was the wrong Tess. I wasn't the one being asked to open for him and go to comedy festivals. Just the one being congratulated and yelled at. It made the already profound disappointment worse.

By the way, after taking my "extra year to develop" when I called the festival the following year I couldn't get an audition because they didn't want to keep showing the execs the "same old people."

It was also around this time that I asked a homeless man what to do with my life.

I had gone into the park to do a quick hike before starting my day working on projects that were bound to go nowhere. I don't know if it was because it was early in the morning or because my head had been up my ass or because I was worried about my future, but I took the wrong path. I ended up on this really steep incline with loose dirt and no way to get a footing. Except that by the time I realized it was going to be impossible to go any farther, I also realized I had gone too far and getting down at that point was equally tricky. Which is also pretty much how I ended up in LA. I figured that if I was going to have a struggle in both directions, I might as well finish at the top. (Which would be a nice metaphor for LA as well, but the jury is still out as to where exactly on that treacherous path I am.)

I made it to the top, continued on a little farther, and then retreated, this time the easy way. When I got back to the spot where I had taken the shortcut, a homeless man sitting on a bench directly across from the incline called out to me. "I didn't think you had it in you."

Maybe the homeless man would like to see me in another year after I've had time to develop.

I smiled, demure like a lady in a Brontë novel (a lady now covered in dirt and God knows what else) and explained, "I bit off more than I could chew."

"Are you a Sagittarius?"

"No." I waited for him to guess my sign because surely, I think, he is magical. As I examine him further I become convinced that I have met Merlin here in these woods, with his long gray beard and mystical way of trying to pick up young girls by guessing their sign. This also, by the way, describes many men in Hollywood who aren't magical.

"Libra," I finally sigh and continue on my unmagical way. Then I think maybe this is the opportunity, the sign I have been waiting for. I walk back to where he is sitting, careful to allow a distance of about ten feet between us, because while I am mystical I am still practical enough to allow for enough space to give me a head start should I have to run from him.

I take a deep breath and look him right in the eye, focusing all my newfound mystical energy on him.

"Where should I move to?" I ask him. I am miserable in LA. I hate the constant feeling that I'm going nowhere, both on the highway and in my own life. I would move somewhere, if I knew of some place where I had a chance of working in entertainment or wouldn't feel like I had just given up. I don't want to live in LA. But I don't want to live anywhere else, either. I'm stuck and I don't know what to do about it, which is the worst feeling,

"Where should I move to?"

"I can't tell you that."

Let me be clear. It wasn't a mystical ominous "I can't tell you that..." followed by a cryptic yet prophetic answer of the sort that may have satisfied me, like "But you'll get a message after the first full moon." Instead it was a "Who is this crazy girl asking me for advice when obviously I'm not exactly the voice of reason drinking out of a paper bag at eight in the morning?"

So yeah, a lot wasn't working out. At this rate, Scientology was right around the corner.

But at least I had a friend who saw the same hallucinations of bruises on a woman's thighs as I did.

In an attempt to attract actual audience members to a coffee-house comedy show on a Saturday night, I created theme nights. On one night it was "Oh, Canada," because it featured all Canadian comics. Apparently, I thought I could fill the audience with INS agents. Heather was dating a guy who I had once called "Young Sort of Good Looking Comic Who Had Everything Going for Him But Would Eventually Squander It All and Piss Everyone Off and Leave Town a Bloated Dick or Dick for Short" but who had turned into much less of a dick since he began dating Heather, another reason I liked her. "Dick" was from Canada and on the show that night, which meant Heather and I got to hang out and drink bad coffee-shop wine.

It was a great show. Since none of the guys who booked comedy shows were from Canada, all of the comics on the show were genuinely funny and not just there because I was being blackmailed into giving them stage time. It also may have been our most well-attended show to date, given one comic's popularity with Canadians who frequent the International Youth Hostel on Hollywood Boulevard.

When the show is over, we're all in a mood. It was a good show, a fun night, and—probably because it was the first time I had left the coffee shop not feeling defeated—I don't want it to end. And neither does anyone else. Heather has brought a friend, a sad, perpetually lonely agent named Louise. Dick is talking to two of the other comics from the show,

Shane and Mick, about the old days starting in Saskatoon or Saskatchewan or Ottawa. We stand out on the sidewalk until The Boyfriend suggests we all move to the Improv bar.

I had loved hanging out at the Improv in those days, because you could walk in by yourself and never spend a moment alone all night. You never had to make a plan with anyone when you went there. Comics drifted in and out all night, doing a set, trying to do a set, or just seeing who else was there. Agents and managers came in to watch clients or find new ones. There were always people there you wanted to catch up with. And even if you didn't, there was at least someone to talk to until someone you wanted to talk to more walked in. We called it "Improv Eyes," when you were talking to someone who never once looked you in the face but rather gazed at the door and around the room looking for someone more important to walk in. But most of the people you were happy to see and were good for filling out thirty minutes of conversation and if you ran into six of them you had an evening.

This night was like that. By the time we all got there the night was in full swing, with the second show having just started. I switch from crappy wine to rum and Cokes, a habit that had evolved since my rum and ginger ale experiment in Vegas. I am convinced this is going to make me sick after the wine, but for some reason I maintain the right amount of buzz throughout the night as we run into all of our favorite people.

Finally, Eddie, the bartender, tells us it's closing. We stand on the sidewalk: The Boyfriend, me, Dick, Heather, Louise, Shane, Mick. We can't stay here but we don't want to go home.

"Let's all go back to our place," The Boyfriend says.

Here's the only problem with this: it's after closing. This means that the liquor stores will no longer be selling alcohol, nor will the grocery store or the 7-Eleven, places they will actually let you buy alcohol in California. These were lean times; looking back I'm not sure how we paid for the alcohol we had already consumed that night. We weren't in the habit of cellaring wine back then. If there were alcohol in the house, it was because it was getting drunk that night, not because we were holding on to it until it was "drinking well." This meant that there was no alcohol in the house for us or our guests to drink, and no way of getting any.

We quickly conferred with our guests. We all lived near enough to each other in Hollywood that everyone would simply go home first, take whatever alcohol they had, and meet back at our place.

Here's what's amazing about that night: everyone showed up. I can't tell you why not one of our guests didn't think to themselves, "I'm home. Why don't I drink what alcohol I have left and call it a night? Why am I going to someone else's house and letting them drink what's left of my shitty, earthquake kit booze?"

But no one did. The Boyfriend and I went home to clean our underwear off the floor and within twenty minutes everyone showed up with what they could forage. It was the "Land of Misfit Booze" to be sure. Someone brought what was left of a bottle of cheap, supermarket red wine. There was a bottle of cherry liqueur. A half-empty bottle of what I think was brandy, that I neither drank nor threw out until we eventually moved . . . and a six-pack of beer. For seven people, three of whom are *Canadian*. But we made it work. We are like Jews with oil at Hanukkah; somehow it all lasts and someday they will write a song about us.

Despite switching back to crappy wine from rum, I still feel OK. We're sitting on the balcony and smoking cigarettes, annoying our neighbors. It's sometime after two in the morning when I notice The Boyfriend is busy in the kitchen.

"What are you doing?"

"I'm making chili."

"But that's the stuff we bought to make chili for dinner tomorrow."

"Yeah, but I want some now. I'll buy more tomorrow."

The Boyfriend makes an amazing chili, which we can now say with accuracy is famous from coast to coast. He started perfecting it once we had moved to LA and the lack of stand-up work had provided him with a) the time to make chili and b) the necessity to cook at home. One of the many unique things about his chili is that there are no tomatoes in it because I'm allergic. And yet it is the deep red color of bricks or blood. No one ever turned down a dinner invitation if chili was on the menu. His chili was requested at Oscar parties, Super Bowl parties, on New Year's Eve. We fed everyone: comics, agents, managers, writers, actors, aestheticians. And chili was one of the easiest ways to feed a lot of people for not a lot of money.

I think it became comfort food, not just for us, but for our friends who frequented our house for dinner, too. The Friday night after September 11, we had a bunch of friends come over. Because two of the flights had been from Boston to LA, there had been a panic among Boston comics, who frequently traveled back home to make money. We all got busy calling each other to make sure they were OK and not traveling. Once we reached someone, we would trade names of everyone else who had been accounted for. That Friday after the candlelight vigil on Hollywood Boulevard, my instinct was to invite a bunch of friends over for chili. I sought a communal experience, and what's more communal than sharing a meal? We all needed something warm that filled us. I think even the nature of chili, everything coming together in one pot, was symbolic of what we were all feeling that week.

So, The Boyfriend started cooking chili. By now, we were all hungry and no one seemed to mind the idea of hanging out for another hour until it was finished. Somewhere in all of this Shane and Louise start making out. It is a completely incongruous match; she is rigid and snobbish, he a sloppy comic with zero responsibilities. But we are all breaking free of our patterns that night. The Boyfriend is serving people the food we had set aside for tomorrow, which necessitates him spending more money for food and a trip to the grocery store on a Sunday, two things he hates. Dick's not being as much of a dick. I'm mixing wine and liquor. It's three in the morning. We all could have gone home five hours ago after LA kicked us all in the ego by forcing ten- and twelve- and seventeen-year comedy veterans into performing in front of twenty-two people in a coffee shop and being grateful for it. But that night we kicked LA back. You are not going to defeat me tonight, LA. Tonight I will take advantage of all your city has to offer . . . or at least all it has to offer between Santa Monica Boulevard and Melrose. Tonight we are not six broke comedians, three of whom might get deported. We are not one sad, lonely agent. We are seven people who have come together to drink and eat chili into the wee hours of the morning.

When the chili was ready, we ladled it into bowls, each of us walking around the apartment marveling at the taste of it. It's three o'clock in the morning and yet all we can talk about is how good the cheese tastes (it's extra sharp aged Wisconsin cheddar) and what's that flavor I can't quite place. (It's pepperoni.) We knew enough to appreciate how the small details like good ingredients could affect the quality of the food. They were things we splurged on when we knew it would make a difference; it was a reflection of the people we aspired to be someday. Or maybe it was just proof of who we've always been.

Tip

Spontaneity is always a useful quality as a hostess. It will help you to cope with the turkey that's done two hours too soon, the weird date your co-worker brings when you never told him he could invite one, and it will enable you to experience some memorable parties you may have otherwise missed hosting.

Recipe

The Boyfriend's Chili: The Colonic You Can Drink With

Ingredients

Olive oil

1 large onion

2 pounds ground beef

2 hot sausage links

2 cups water

1 12-ounce beer

4 teaspoons paprika

2 tablespoons plus 2 teaspoons cumin

1 cup chili powder

2 teaspoons cayenne pepper

8 cloves garlic, minced

2 tablespoons white vinegar

1 15oz.-can black beans, rinsed and drained
1 15oz.-can kidney beans, rinsed and drained
1 15oz.-can pinto beans, rinsed and drained
2 inches pepperoni, cut into small pieces
Salt, pepper, and Tabasco to taste
Cheddar cheese
Sour cream
Chopped tomatoes (optional)

The Boyfriend has been making this recipe for years, largely by heart, which means he often changes things up and doesn't measure accurately, preferring to adjust his spices to taste. So, if you are worried about it being too spicy, use only half or so of the spices at first, adding as you go along to your own desired flavor.

Heat oil in a large stew pot. Dice the onion, then sauté it for 5 minutes over medium heat in the pot. When the onion starts to brown, add the ground beef. Keep "chopping" the beef with a wooden spoon so the beef breaks up into little pieces, which is how The Boyfriend likes it best, just tiny granules of beef. Once the beef is browned and chopped into the preferred consistency, add water, beer, beans, paprika, cumin, chili powder, cayenne pepper, vinegar, and garlic. In a separate pan, sauté the sausage and then add that to the chili pot, as well. Bring to a boil, then reduce to a simmer. Continue to simmer for 2 hours, stirring it every so often so it doesn't stick to the bottom and make sure the liquid isn't boiling off. If it does, add more beer or water.

At the start of the second hour, dice up the pepperoni into ¼ to ½ inch cubes. "Don't be anal about it," says The

Boyfriend. "They don't have to be perfect cubes. Just don't make them too big." Sear the pepperoni in a pan with a little oil and add it to the chili. Now's a good time to start tasting and adjusting the spices, too. If it's too hot, add more water. If it's not hot enough, add Tabasco or more cayenne pepper. Continue to simmer for the second hour.

Serve with cheese, sour cream, and chopped tomatoes.

When we want to be healthy we substitute dark ground turkey instead of beef. You could use ground white turkey, but it's dryer and we don't want to be that healthy. Conversely, when we want to just stop our hearts for an afternoon we use only 1½ pounds of ground meat *and* ½ a pound of stewing beef, which we let cook until it starts to fall apart. Also, you can add an 8-ounce can of tomato sauce or tomato paste to thicken your chili, but we don't since I can't eat tomatoes.

Chapter 5
How to Count Your Blessings

We had been in LA long enough now that we knew people who had houses. And while I still desired to entertain in my own home, even I had to admit that it was silly to cram fifteen people for Thanksgiving dinner into our 650 square feet. So this year I was cooking some of my standards, but bringing them to our friend Nessa's house. She had a house. I was very jealous.

When I think back on my old daydreams about having a house—or at least a bigger apartment—they were always inspired by entertaining; parties I would throw, people I would have over for dinner, the meals I would cook. I would make plans with friends who had bigger places and feel limited in what we could do. What I really wanted to do was invite them over. But it seemed silly to make people who had a much bigger place spend the evening eating in my tiny apartment where the dining room, kitchen, living room, and office was the same three-hundred-square-foot space of open floor plan. It was one thing in college or those first few years out. We all lived in similar situations; we were all in the same place. But as more peers moved to bigger dwellings, entertaining at my place seemed pointless. What was worse, it underlined my feeling that others were moving forward and I wasn't.

So we were going to Nessa's and while I would still get to cook everything I loved—apple pies, turkey cut out cookies, and my goat cheese and wild rice stuffing—I would be spared from having to cram twelve people around two desks pushed together.

The night before Thanksgiving, we went by the Improv. This was one of my favorite nights of the year to stop by. The Improv was the only comedy club in town that had its own separate bar and restaurant. None of the other clubs had a place where comics could just hang, without having to actually walk into the club itself. This meant that in order to get in, you had to first go through some douchebag door guy of the week who was trying to get a $15 cover charge out of you. Maybe it wasn't fifteen. Maybe it was ten. Maybe it was five. Whatever it was, it was money I didn't have. Two of these clubs were on Sunset Boulevard where I couldn't even afford to park. So, the alternative was to explain that you were a comic.

My first spot ever at the Improv, the manager explained to us that there were twenty thousand comics in Los Angeles. I used to think he was exaggerating for comedic purposes. Now, I know he was underestimating.

So, the way to "hang out" in these clubs if you didn't want to pay the cover charge was to say, "Hello, my good man. My name is Tess Rafferty and I hail from Old Beantown where I used to dazzle seven people in a Chinese restaurant on Sunday nights with my jokes. Won't you please let me in so that I might treat your fine establishment to more of the same?" The door guys don't give a crap about me after the likes of three Wayans brothers, Dane Cook, and a Sarah Silverman just walked in, but because the Improv had a bar, you could walk in without having to contemplate your own anonymity. Not that there wasn't plenty of time to do that while you sat there.

Most nights of the year, the club was filled with "industry showcases." A bunch of guys wearing the same suit having expense-account drinks while they talked and otherwise looked bored as comics tried their hardest to be the next thing. The bar was packed with comics not on the showcases, looking to talk to each other, schmooze the men in similar suits, and run into the club and fill up the back when a comics' favorite came out to do a spot, like Mitch Hedberg or Zach Galifianakis.

There were no Men in the Same Suit the night before Thanksgiving. Instead, it was filled with people who couldn't—or didn't want to—go home. People talked about what they were doing for the holiday, instead of what they were doing in Hollywood. It was also free from a lot of bullshit as there was no one important left in town to schmooze, so you could actually have a conversation with people you liked and not worry that one of you was going to leave halfway to talk to someone who could, but probably wouldn't, do something for you.

On this night in particular, I was setting up two friends; a recent widow and a mild-mannered writer who hit it off but never made it out for a second date because the two of them kept getting alternately sick for the next three months. Perhaps they had too much in common. Into the bar walked

Semi-Closeted TV Actor, another comic we knew who now had a successful TV show and a horrible drinking problem. I say semi-closeted, because while it was not out to the world at large that he was gay, it was common knowledge among everyone in comedy and something he never tried to hide socially. He also had a rotating entourage of young straight male comedians who had just moved to town, excited that the guy they were fans of from "that thing" wanted to be their friend and help them out. The other comics gossiped about how "mutually beneficial" it was to them both, and while it was always just gossip, the following was an exchange that I can bear witness to from the day after Thanksgiving the previous year.

Semi-Closeted TV Actor walks into the bar.

TESS

How was your Thanksgiving?

SEMI-CLOSETED TV ACTOR

Great!

TESS

What did you do?

SEMI-CLOSETED TV ACTOR

Not much. We just hung out, watched basketball, had sex, ordered a couple of pizzas.

TESS

Fun!

Semi-Closeted TV Actor heads to the bar. A moment later New in Town Male Comic walks in.

                    TESS
Hi! How was your Thanksgiving? What did you
do?

                    NEW IN TOWN MALE COMIC
I hung out at Semi-Closeted TV Actor's Place.

                    TESS
Oh. (beat.) Just the two of you?

                    NEW IN TOWN MALE COMIC
Yeah.

                    TESS
Oh. (beat.) All day?

                    NEW IN TOWN MALE COMIC
Yup.

                    TESS
No one else?

                    NEW IN TOWN MALE COMIC
Nope.

                    TESS
Oh. (beat.) Fun!

Only this night at the Improv, as I made the rounds talking to various comics in the Young, Straight, and New in Town Entourage, it was clear no one was spending their Thanksgiving having sex and watching basketball. One by one they told me their plans of going to relatives' or other friends or flying home in the morning. I realized that Semi-Closeted TV Actor would be spending the holiday alone.

We had invited him over for Thanksgiving in years past, not that we expected him to come. We had neither sex nor pizza to offer him. But year after year we made the invitation and he said in his charming way that won him TV roles, "There's no place I would rather be." And this was my first LA lesson that someone could be lying to you and you could know they were lying and they could know that you knew that they were lying, and yet you both just smiled and pretended it was going to happen.

I know people who don't live in LA think it's the capital of fake and Satan's primary residence, the one he lists on his tax returns, but it's not that different from the rest of the world. Let's say you're on your way home from work one night and all you want to do is hit the grocery store and grab a rotisserie chicken and some ice cream so you can watch *The Mentalist*. Only in the checkout lane you run into someone from high school and you exchange thirty seconds of small talk that feels like an hour because Simon Baker is waiting for you, and what do you say to end it? "We should get together sometime and grab a drink and talk over old times." Are you going to do that? No. And Semi-Closeted TV Actor was not going to come to my house for turkey.

Nevertheless, it is not in our nature to let someone spend a holiday alone, so this year we asked him again if he wanted to come with us. He said maybe and asked us to call him the next day.

The rest of the night passes quickly as we talk to other comics and our friends who we're trying to set up and everything goes smoothly until I get in the car to go home. All of a sudden a wave of nausea and dizziness hits me completely unexpectedly. One minute I was fine, the next minute my equilibrium was off and I had my head out of the window for air, convinced I was going to vomit or fall out of the car. I didn't know what was wrong. I had had no more to drink than normal.

We made the short drive home and I was no better. The Boyfriend made me a grilled-cheese sandwich with sharp Tillamook cheddar on the Foreman Grill, a popular post-Improv snack. At this point I was crawling on the floor because standing up made me too dizzy.

"I think I've been roofied."

"You haven't been roofied. You're just drunk. Eat your grilled-cheese sandwich and go to bed."

I woke up on Thanksgiving morning throwing up and running a fever, two things I never do. I can count on one hand the times in my adult life I have thrown up. Once I babysat a two-year-old and caught whatever she had and once was this day. And once in Boston, I was drinking with The Boyfriend at a local bar after a show. Only he wasn't my boyfriend then, just another comic, and when I stumbled home to my actual boyfriend at the time, I had had so much to drink I found it hilarious to tell him that I was drinking "peanut giorgio," so I kind of deserved that. I also never run fevers since my normal body temperature is sometimes as low as 96.2 degrees, which I think is cause for concern, but my doctors tell me not to worry about. If my temperature ever even gets to 98.6 degrees, I stay home from work. Thus, with the presence of a fever, The Boyfriend started to take me seriously.

By noon I felt well enough to touch other people's food and start cooking. Don't look at me like that. Getting roofied isn't contagious. I also figured Semi-Closeted would be up by then and we should make the obligatory call. I want to be clear: I didn't invite him not wanting him to attend, just not expecting him to. Every time I'd invited him anywhere I always genuinely welcomed his presence. I just knew he'd never come.

I left a message and to my surprise he called back and said he'd love to join us at Nessa's. We knew that he'd been relieved by either the state or his own good judgment of the opportunity to drive, so we offered to pick him up.

We drove north into the hills that overlooked Los Angeles and—on a good day—as far out as Catalina. The farther up the hill we went, past expensive homes and then even more expensive homes, we joked that we could smell money, and then burning money. A general principle of real estate in Los Angeles is that prices increase the farther west you go and the farther into the hills you go and we couldn't believe how high up the hill Semi-Closeted lived.

Suddenly the jokes about money stopped and we were silent for a moment. Finally I said, "Do you feel like we're going to pick up Grandpa?"

"Yeah. I was just thinking that."

At every family gathering there are always the few members who alternate bringing the elderly relative who can no longer drive, but who no one wants to leave at home alone.

There was something melancholy about making that drive that night past those expensive homes to pick up someone who couldn't get around due to a *different* kind of immobility.

We arrived at his home where The S.C. Actor greeted us, beer in hand. He showed us around a beautiful house sporadically, but well, decorated. He stopped at an enormous picture window and we looked out to Catalina. The Boyfriend later said, "I got the feeling that if we had just suggested skipping the party and hanging out there and ordering some pizzas, he would have been perfectly fine with it." He made no mention of offering sex or basketball.

Semi-Closeted got into the back of our car and said it smelled like Thanksgiving, and indeed it did. It was loaded up like Santa's sleigh with wine, and stuffing, and pie, and cookies. Semi-Closeted conversely got into the car with a six-pack of Heineken that had only two beers left in it, which we never saw again. I assumed he drank them in the car during the short drive over.

We arrived at Nessa's where again, he raved about how great it smelled. "It smells like home," he said, which to this day I feel like he was reading off a script. If his home had smelled this good at Thanksgiving, I thought, wouldn't he be there? Look, I'm not judging, I don't go home for Thanksgiving, either. But I'm not the one having a liquid Wild Turkey dinner alone.

He knew a few people there and perhaps that was part of the problem. A couple of guys had been in the Young, Straight, and New in Town Entourage a few years before and were now enjoying the holiday with their girlfriends. Maybe that was why. But in the end, I think it was just a small part of it. After raving about how good everything smelled, he stayed for a short while before calling a cab and leaving, having eaten nothing.

I don't remember much about the rest of the evening, besides the fact that I tried a glass or two of the wine I was looking forward to without vomiting again, which only reinforced my roofie theory because surely I would not have bounced back from a twenty-four-hour bug so quickly. I know the food was delicious and it was too bad that he had none. If there's one thing I've seen eating fantastic meals, it's the sudden joy that can overtake someone when they put a bite of food in their mouth that is unexpectedly delicious. It's the pause, the breath. For that bite they are in the moment. Maybe he would have had that moment. Maybe that food that smelled so good, would have given him a moment to take pleasure in something that money couldn't buy. Maybe it would have put him in the present long enough to stop thinking about everything that was plaguing him from the past. Maybe the laughter that comes with sharing a meal around a dinner table would have given him a sense of community that he so desperately lacked.

He had a house but we had everything.

Tip

Make as many things as you can a day ahead of time because you never know if you're going to get roofied at a bar the night before, which could affect your prep time. And if you don't get roofied, then you have the whole day to relax with a glass of Prosecco and count your blessings.

Recipe

Molasses Cinnamon Bread:
It's What's for Breakfast If
You're Not Vomiting

Ingredients

¾ cup honey

¾ cup molasses

3½ cups flour

2 teaspoons baking soda

2 teaspoons ginger

2 teaspoons allspice

2 teaspoons cinnamon

2 cups milk

Now, technically, this is not "bread." This is a quick bread, which means it's made without yeast. The consistency is more like a muffin that has been put into a loaf pan, but that doesn't mean it's not delicious.

I make this every Thanksgiving, mostly for myself. I find that there's far too much food on the table come dinner for anyone to care about bread. Are you the poor bastard who gets asked to bring rolls to Thanksgiving dinner? You should just throw your five dollars in the trash. Who needs a roll with the cavalcade of carbs marching into your gullet? Who needs bread when you're already eating stuffing—which is made out of bread!

So I make this for me and usually eat it for breakfast the whole holiday weekend. I cut off a slice and toast it or warm it up in the oven and then slather with butter. The smell and flavor is so evocative of this time of year it really helps put me in the holiday spirit. Also, it's super easy.

Mix together ¾ cup of honey and ¾ cup of molasses. People will tell you to mix all of your dry ingredients together, and you can do that if you want, or just do what the lazy people like me do and add them separately. It's 3½ cups of flour, 2 teaspoons baking soda, 2 teaspoons ginger, 2 teaspoons allspice, and 2 teaspoons cinnamon. (I usually add a tiny bit more. I like cinnamon.) Alternate the dry ingredients with 2 cups of milk. When everything is mixed well, pour into a loaf pan and bake at 350°F for approximately 1¼ hours, until a knife inserted in the center comes out clean.

Chapter 6
How to Have a Fun Christmas Party for Adults & Children, and Even the Hosts (Yes, That Means You)

All of a sudden, in the course of one year, everything changed.

About six months after the Thanksgiving at Nessa's, The Boyfriend got his first TV writing job. He'd had his first IRS audit earlier that year, so frankly we were due for some good news. Apparently, a place where he had made about $875 the year before made a few typos on a couple of forms they had submitted to the IRS and reported that instead of $875, he had made $87,500. When he called to tell them what had happened, they sort of laughed it off and said, "You're lucky. Bob's form said he made over two hundred thousand." Yeah. We were lucky.

But he did get a job and a few months after that one ended, another one came up. It looked like he might actually have a writing career, only I still had no idea what was going to become of me. During the first year of his legitimate employment I worked for a skin care company, which was cool because I got free products and often free waxing from the aestheticians who worked there. When that job folded, I lived off unemployment for a while. Then I did some copywriting for some Web-based ad agency that was tedious. They would buy a domain name to drive traffic to a client's Web site, the idea being that they would create a fake Web site and then when you clicked the TELL ME MORE button, you would be redirected to the client's. Each fake site had forty to sixty pages, each page containing certain key words that you had to use a certain number of times. They had a whole science to the word count and key words, which were often highly technical terms like "tool and die machinery" that you were hard pressed to use in one sentence, let alone forty. It paid OK but we parted ways when they wanted all of the copywriters to post a photo of themselves online in order to continue working for them. Frankly that seemed creepy and I was secretly relieved to no longer have to find ways to use the phrase "live call forwarding" in a sentence.

Soon enough I was back to temping again. And then, in a year, everything changed.

January 4, 2005. I left my temp gig early for a job interview on *The Soup,* a pop culture clip show that I had never heard of and was thrilled at the possibility of working on. K.P. was a comic I had known for years. In fact, I had been at his wedding when Heather and I first met and discovered Bruisey Thighs. He had always read my writing and swore that when he got a chance to bring me on to something he would. Now the new head writer, he had asked me to submit. I was nervous writing jokes because I always thought my strengths were in dialogue and scripts, but someone liked them enough to bring me in for an interview—the dullest interview in the history of interviews.

There were five of us in the meeting and the conversation had the tone of a nurse trying to make small talk as she asks you to step on the scale. I think I was the nurse. I was the one trying to find some common ground to put the other person at ease while they were the ones who just wanted to get it over with so they could put their clothes on and get back to work. When it was over, I drove home strangely at peace with the whole thing. It would be OK. I would go back to the temp job tomorrow. It wouldn't be so bad. My life would go on as before. I certainly didn't know any different.

By the time I had gotten home, they called with a job offer. It was half what The Boyfriend made at his first job and that's probably why they were hiring me after that interview, but who cares! I had a job!

It was supposed to last thirteen weeks. But after thirteen we were successful enough that they kept us on. A six-week break in the summer turned into only three when they brought us back early. At that point they said they were leaving us on until the end of the year. And by the end of the year they said we'd be back for the entirety of the next one. And in December of 2005, eleven months after I stopped temping, we bought our first house.

I don't want to say it was the height of the housing boom

in LA; it was more like the week after. But after nearly six years of trying to entertain in that apartment I didn't care. I was getting a house and I was getting one by Christmas.

Two years later even more has changed. The Boyfriend has become so successful as a writer that he has become a Writers Guild of America member and they are now on strike. Every morning he wakes up at six and drives to Warner Brothers where he walks in a circle for four hours holding a sign. As I wasn't a union member and my show wasn't a WGA show, I was still working, so things weren't so bad for us. Many other people we knew, however, weren't so lucky. For many of our friends the sole bread winner, or sometimes both bread winners, were in the union and thus not working. It was a contentious time for people, too. People who worked in production were put out of work by the strike and were extremely resentful. Also, some writers who were in the union but had nonunion jobs kept working. This was a huge source of anger as both sides debated it back and forth. Even among the striking writers, there were disagreements over what they were fighting for and how it was being handled. There was no joy in Mudville and now it was Christmas.

The holiday party season is competitive. You have to get out ahead of everyone else and announce your event, so as to lock in your guest list as soon as possible. Otherwise you risk people who are already committed or worse—double booked. I am not a fan of the double bookers, and in fact we don't allow it at all on Thanksgiving. If you are double booked, it means that you have a plan for the evening that looks good on paper but that is never going to work in real life. You are either going to get to my place first, anxious that you will never make it to the second party in time and leave before the fun starts or you are going to come by second, probably late, because you were late getting to the first party and then you got lost getting from there to here. We finally put our foot down for Thanksgivings because it is impossible to plan an elaborate sit-down dinner when your guests are popping in and out, and what kind of fat ass are you anyway that you need two turkey dinners?

So even though it was only two days after Thanksgiving, we were busy ironing out the details for our holiday event so that we could send the Evite out that weekend. We decided on a Sunday afternoon gathering, in order to further remove ourselves from the competition, and then we made the hardest choice of all . . . we decided to include children.

I don't like children at parties. I don't like them at my parties, and I don't like them at yours, either. I think parties should be adult affairs. Childless couples don't want to be around your kids and most people with kids that I know, are thrilled to have a few hours off from theirs and everyone else's. I can't swear around your children. I can't talk loudly about sex around your children. I can't get drunk around your children. And I certainly can't say, "Get the fuck off my very expensive, brand-new cabinets!" to your children. That's your job. Or at least it's supposed to be. But most parents I know are either too overly indulgent to reprimand their children, or refuse to because they are secretly mad at me for mastering the art of birth control. (I said "most," Dear Friends Reading This Book. Of course I don't mean you.)

But it was Christmas. I love Christmas. I love Christmas more than any childless woman who doesn't believe in God should. And for years when I was unemployed, I had plenty of time to love Christmas. I made my own cards. I decorated every square inch of our 650-square-foot apartment. And I baked. I made sugar cookies and cut them out in the shapes of all things Christmas, and then I decorated them. Sometimes I had friends over with their children to decorate them. Sometimes I made The Boyfriend decorate them. And lots of times I decorated them for hours alone.

Given that our party was on a Sunday afternoon we knew it would be hard for our friends to find a sitter, especially during the holidays, and that some of them actually liked spending time with their kids anyway. So we decided to invite the kids, too, and our solution to what we would do with them was cookies. We'll have the parents over for cocktails and the kids can decorate cookies. We had just been up to Santa Barbara wine country, and I had found the perfect Syrah to serve. It was a great big spicy red, perfect for the holidays. In addition to that, we'd serve Irish coffees, the way they make them in Ireland where we had just gone that summer. We'd have hot chocolate for the kids.

In addition to the sugar and alcohol and caffeine, The Boyfriend wanted to smoke some meat. When we bought the house, we had agreed to hold onto a smoker for a friend, since we now had space in our garage. We had used the smoker all of once and the results weren't encouraging, although I suppose not bad for two guys who had no idea what they were doing. The Boyfriend thought he could improve upon the last time and was anxious to find an opportunity to try again. He thought this party should be the time.

I had my reservations, but the preparations proceeded as planned. The day before the party we were going to have to get our tree and at least put the lights on it. Also, I would have to make the cookies then, too. The whip cream for the coffees I could do the morning of, along with the icing. I would get the old drip coffeepot down (we mostly used a French press these days) and leave a pot of coffee hot all day. The only thing I wasn't sure how it would work was the hot chocolate.

I wanted to serve homemade hot chocolate, being philosophically opposed to instant. Not only do I think it tastes like hot water with artificial sweetener and dirt in it, but I am turned off by the idea of putting all of those chemicals, those corn syrup solids and hydrogenated diglycerides, into one's body as well. Anthrax is a powder that comes in an envelope, too. The problem was, I couldn't figure out how to keep it hot all day. It seemed like overkill to pick up one of those industrial, AA-meeting coffee urns. Keeping the hot chocolate warm in a pot on the stove all day seemed like it would just burn on the bottom and get a film on top. Williams-Sonoma sold just the contraption for this sort of occasion (wouldn't they, though?) but it seemed like a silly investment for something I would use once a year.

But the thing was The Boyfriend had given me a hot chocolate cookbook the Christmas before, and the recipes were pretty remarkable: Mexican hot chocolate, malted hot chocolate, maple whiskey hot chocolate. If there were going to be kids in my house getting my furniture sticky, they were at least going to leave with an appreciation for finer foods (and whiskey).

The Thursday night before the party I was still debating what to do as I drove home from work with my now boss, K.P. I was mulling over the problem with him as we discussed the pros and cons of throwing a party and the stresses of party prep. Whereas I had planned this party three weeks ago, K.P. was still deciding whether or not to throw one the following week. We're different people.

"The thing is," I began, "I'm the only one who's going to care that the hot chocolate is not homemade, and I'm not even going to be drinking it. I'm going to be drinking wine."

"Yeah, so what are you doing?"

What was I doing? And that's when I was hit with the kind of Zen clarity that many hostesses may never achieve even if they spend their entire lives throwing parties in a Buddhist monastery. It was like I had a crystal ball. And I was able to look into it and see into the future. I looked at my house the afternoon of the party and saw nothing but half-drunk cups of gourmet hot chocolate whose very expensive ingredients were now getting cold and clumpy. I had never seen a child finish a cup of hot chocolate, even when I was a child. No, instead of melting down bittersweet chocolate in a double boiler and whisking in heavy cream, I was going to set out a decorative basket of hot chocolate packets next to the teapot on the stove and let their parents deal with it. Determined to not waste any more time or money on the matter, I decided I wouldn't even buy the hot chocolate, I would just steal some from the break room at work.

That matter settled, the conversation turned toward the upcoming weekend. K.P. and his wife needed to go out and buy gifts for their four-year-old daughter some day that weekend, preferably when the four-year-old daughter they were buying gifts for wouldn't be around. Since we were going to be home all day Saturday prepping for the party anyway, I agreed to watch her.

Now I know this may seem odd, given everything that I

have said above about children, but let me explain. First of all, I don't mind children at times when you have agreed to see them. I don't hate children: I mostly hate their parents who refuse to discipline them, bring them places where it's not appropriate, and have become people I no longer recognize since they had them. Second of all, K.P.'s daughter wasn't an asshole. She was a really good kid who liked to help and I was excited for the opportunity to make Christmas cookies with a child for the afternoon without having to put her through college or hear how much she hates me in ten years.

So there we were on Saturday afternoon: the Child, The Boyfriend, myself, and Frank. Frank was our cat. We had a cat now, too. A lot had changed. When we moved into our house we inherited a feral cat colony that we slowly tried to trap, neuter, and release or place if the cats were young enough. Born in the backyard earlier that year, Frank wandered into the house one day and decided that we had things pretty good on the inside, and began splitting his time between there and the backyard ever since.

The Child and I were in the kitchen, covered in flour from rolling out the cookies: I in a pair of old sweatpants that had so many holes The Boyfriend kept insisting I throw them out, she in an old Duran Duran shirt of mine. The Boyfriend was similarly attired in cargo shorts and a Framingham State sweatshirt, despite having never gone to Framingham State. He was busy hanging lights on the tree so that we could get it decorated for the party the next day.

And that's when the doorbell rang.

Looking out on the front porch I see our friends Becky and Patrick, dressed in their holiday party finest, a festively arranged plate of brownie bars in their hands. I quickly called to The Boyfriend that we had guests as I went to answer the door.

"Hiiiiiiii...!" we all said too enthusiastically, as we realized what was happening and yet still tried to make it OK for each other.

"Come in," I said and just like that I looked down on the ground and noticed a puddle of green puke the same color as the fresh Christmas tree.

In the four or five months we had had him, Frank had never thrown up. Come to think of it, as we had only had him for a few months, I don't think Becky and Patrick even knew we had a cat yet.

"There's a lot going on here," I said as I ran to get a towel to clean up the puke.

They were embarrassed to get the date wrong. We were horrified that good friends saw us looking like this. So we did what came naturally. We offered them a drink.

We grabbed a couple of glasses off the bar and popped open the wine they had brought and settled back into the area of the house we had named "Wine Corner." Suddenly, another party was heard from.

"Tess, I finished them all!"

Oh, Jesus Christ, the Child! During this entire scene, which felt like an eternity but was really much shorter, the Child had been diligently working away in the kitchen, cutting out shapes of stars and trees and bells.

"I forgot to mention there's a child here," I explained as I filled up my glass.

Fortunately, we had just bought this piece of art that was largely made up of magnets and the Child was learning to count, and so she amused herself counting and playing with magnets while the four of us had a healthy glass of wine and forgot our common mortification. We talked about the upcoming holidays, their family gift exchange back in Wisconsin, and whether or not I could expect Frank to vomit the entire Christmas season. At the bottom of the glass they left, and we returned to prepping and babysitting.

The Child's parents arrived to pick her up, another round of drinks was poured, and by the time they left we were still in holey sweatpants and a Framingham State sweatshirt. We had a tree to finish decorating and a roast in the fridge that The Boyfriend was determined to smoke the next day, despite the fact that it had to be started first thing in the morning and monitored all day.

Again, I looked into the Crystal Ball.

"We can't do this," I started, "there's not enough time and you are going to drive yourself crazy trying to do it. Let's put the roast in the oven tomorrow. We can slow roast it at a low temp and then we'll have something to eat when everyone leaves around five."

It took some convincing, but eventually The Boyfriend abandoned his overdeveloped sense of responsibility ("But I said there would be smoked meat. I can't not have smoked meat.") and agreed. We sent out an e-mail explaining to everyone that there would be no smoked meat tomorrow, but that we were pretty sure they were coming for the alcohol anyway.

The day of our holiday party dawned a crisp 75 degrees, presenting yet another case for not serving homemade hot chocolate to children. My Winter Wonderland–themed holiday extravaganza necessitated the air-conditioning and short sleeves. Still, I persevered, brewing the coffee and whipping the whip cream. I mixed some confectioners' sugar with milk, dividing it into separate bowls and adding a variety of food coloring. I then put a tablecloth down on the table and as much newspaper as I could aesthetically stand on the floor. Kids and icing could get messy. When we moved out of the apartment two years before, the movers lifted the couch off the floor and found underneath it a cookie frosted pink and in the shape of an Easter egg. It was December.

"You have kids?" the mover asked me.

"Nope. Just friends . . . ," I replied.

". . . Who don't watch their kids," I thought.

People started to arrive and here was the cool thing: people brought food. After the e-mail that said we weren't smoking meat because we had run out of time, people went ahead and brought stuff. Some picked up meats on the way over. Others brought leftovers from home. Someone else brought a pizza.

When I looked around I saw single friends talking to friends who were holding their new babies. I saw childless friends decorating cookies. I saw no one drinking hot chocolate. Two gay friends were coveting my magnetic art piece. My party was a hit. And no one was talking about the strike. I saw parents, excited to have someplace to bring their kids for the afternoon, sitting at the table, patiently helping their kids with the cookies and frosting, and most importantly, watching them. All except for one.

In the kitchen Tara was having a glass of wine, explaining to another friend that her kids were in the other room. "But I'm in here because I get too anxious when I'm watching them."

Of course, it makes *you* much too anxious to actually watch *your* children, thus ensuring their safety. It will give you much more peace of mind to hang somewhere where you can't see what dangers in which they might be putting themselves, or my furniture.

Five o'clock came and went. People were still walking in the door. The kids sat sugar stoned in front of the TV watching *Elf.* A gay couple blew off their second party to stay at ours. My party was the event of the season! The roast was now finished and since no one was leaving, The Boyfriend wandered around with it on a cutting board, cutting off slices for people. We tried a brand-new coffee rub on the outside of the beef, and the spices combined with the meat were perfect for the weather, which was finally starting to cool. This party was everything we had wanted it to be and the best part was, we had eliminated unnecessary work that would have only left us stressed.

I walk out to the back patio where some friends are smoking, to tell them that there's some pretty awesome meat if they want it. We sit and chat for a moment when Tara's three-year-old daughter walks out from behind the gate that surrounds the pool. For those of you who don't know, a pool is a large body of water in a cement hole that small, unattended children can drown in.

We hurry the girl inside and I make a mental note to never invite Tara to another gathering with her children.

Five years later, I have kept that promise to myself. I also still have those same hot chocolate packets in my pantry.

Tip

The easiest way to alleviate stress while planning a party is to eliminate things that you receive no benefit from. Are you stressed because you have no lemons cut up for the bar, but you don't even like lemon in your cocktails? Then you don't need lemons. Never forget, this is your show. Do only what you personally will appreciate later, and remember: children never appreciate anything.

Recipe
Sugar Cookies & Frosting: Minutes of Entertainment for Hyperactive Children

Ingredients

3 sticks butter
¼ cup sugar
1 box plus 1 cup confectioners' sugar
3 cups flour
½ teaspoon vanilla
½ teaspoon salt
Milk
Food coloring
Vanilla? (see recipe)

I used to have something of a cookie cutter problem. I spent years collecting cookie cutters. I wasn't content to just have ones for Christmas, I needed bunnies for Easter, and turkeys for Thanksgiving, too. I wanted shamrocks. I bought wineglass cookie cutters and ones shaped like a bunch of grapes. Did I mention, the pumpkins, cats, and bats for Halloween? The reindeer shapes that, when assembled, make a 3-D replica of Santa's sleigh? It was getting out of hand. If you don't believe me, ask yourself how many women have a cookie cutter drawer in their kitchen. How many women made it a design feature when they remodeled their kitchen?

The dough is easy. You can handle the dough, right? Cream together 3 sticks of butter with ¼ cup of sugar and 1 cup of confectioners' sugar. Add to that 3 cups of flour, ½ teaspoon vanilla, and ½ teaspoon salt. Roll the dough into a ball or a log, wrap well in plastic wrap, being sure to coat the plastic lightly with flour so the dough doesn't stick, and refrigerate for 4 to 6 hours.

Sometimes when you take the dough out of the fridge, it needs a few minutes to warm up to a rollable temp. Too warm and it spreads too easily and doesn't maintain its shape as well, but too cold and you'll have a tough go of it. This is trial and error. If it's too cold initially, walk away for 5 or 10 minutes, do those dishes that are piling up or your makeup, and come back and try again.

Break off a ball of the dough and roll out onto a floured surface with a rolling pin or your 20-ounce beer bottle from chapter 2. Be sure to flour both the surface you put the dough on and the top of your dough as well. Roll the dough out to about ½ an inch and then start cutting out your shapes. If you've used enough flour on the surface and the dough isn't too soft, you should have no trouble lifting the shapes right off the counter and onto the baking sheet. Bake at 325°F for 20 minutes, or whenever the cookies are done to your liking. Let them cool before decorating, otherwise the icing will run all over the place getting little hands sticky right before they sit on your new couch.

In a big bowl mix together a box of confectioners' sugar and some milk, until it gets to a good icing consistency. If you put too much milk in, add more sugar. You can also throw some vanilla in there, but after you see how many half-eaten cookies the children leave behind, ask yourself what's the point? My advice is to get the icing to consistency and taste you like. Screw the children.

Divide the icing into separate bowls or cups and then go nuts with food coloring. Sure, do your reds and greens for Christmas, or your orange and yellow for Halloween, but then do purple and blue and pink, too; anything to keep them occupied. Throw out some containers of sprinklers and after putting a generous layer of newspaper on your table and floor, you may have a chance of having a conversation with one of your friends before their kids start crying.

Chapter 7
How to Serve a Specialty Drink with an Iron Fist

It started like many things do: I wanted to show off.

I had just perfected my braised lamb shank and I thought everyone should know it. So a few weeks after our Cookie Decorating Party, I was cooking Christmas Eve dinner for two of my best friends and their husbands.

Months before we had been sitting in my backyard on Girls' Night, a weekly ritual where we ordered sushi, drank a lot of wine, and then watched *America's Next Top Model* since I had to cover it for work. In between, we discussed who at our jobs were trying to thwart us and aired our most recent grievances about our partners.

In the last few years Lois and Edie had become my two closest confidantes. I had met Lois out at a show one night. We had many friends in common and technically had met once before, but *that* night something was different; she told me I had good arms. A friendship was born.

Within weeks, Lois and I were meeting regularly for cheese plates and wine flights at a French bistro. We lived close to each other and seemed to be up for the same kind of fun; namely, eating great things, drinking good wine, and talking about boys. We fell right in step together and when we both said simultaneously, apropos of nothing, "I want to go to London," it seemed like kismet and Lois spearheaded a trip. Within months we were enjoying our third round of drinks at the Wolfgang Puck inside the International terminal at LAX.

Edie and Lois had known each other for years, being part of the same circle through which I had met Lois. Within a year of meeting Lois, Edie and I were showing up at the same gatherings often enough that we were eventually making plans on our own. Edie was a redhead from the South although she had lived in LA long enough to have partied with the Red Hot Chili Peppers when they still did things like party. Needless to say she was always up for a drink and she had the same blunt sense of humor that Lois and I shared.

Lois asked what we were doing for the holidays. Once she determined we were all staying in town, Lois invited us for Thanksgiving and I offered to host everyone for Christmas. I had abandoned Christmas at our families' houses about five years earlier. The first few years The Boyfriend and I made an annual pilgrimage back East where we would spend two weeks bouncing around between Boston to see our friends, and Long Island and Delaware to see our families. Our families lived just close enough that it would be rude not to see both of them, which is to say not close at all. It was a four-or five-hour drive and every time we packed up the car on

Christmas morning we were torn between the hassle of leaving and the hassle of staying.

Finally one fall I just decided I was done. Whereas I used to always look forward to the trip despite the hassle, this year I just felt I couldn't get on that plane one more time. I didn't want to fight the crowds and pack for two weeks and still not have adequate winter clothes and worry about shipping gifts and sleep in guest rooms or on couches and never have any alone time. I didn't want to go.

One of the last times we went back, we spent a couple of days with friends in Maine. The house was a brisk 55 degrees. For them it was normal; for us it was the temperature at which you keep the wine fridge. We didn't want to shower because we couldn't bear the moment between getting out of the shower and getting into our clothes. At night, The Boyfriend was so cold he couldn't sleep. The blankets weren't enough. He had on a sweatshirt, too, but no pants to wear except for his jeans. Desperate times call for desperate cross-dressing measures. We had to dig into the bag of Christmas gifts from the L.L.Bean outlet store, so he could put on the pink snowflake pajama bottoms I had bought for my aunt.

That may have been the low point.

Yes, the more I thought about waking up in my own bed on Christmas, and the day after that, the more I wanted to stay. Plus, one of the drawbacks to spending the holiday at someone else's home, for me, was not being able to celebrate the way I wanted to. I wanted to plan the menu and make the food and serve the meal at whatever time I wanted. Everyone I stayed with was always very accommodating about letting me help and make things but the fact of the matter is: I like to be in control.

So it's no surprise that when Lois e-mailed us within the week to say that, unbeknownst to her, her husband had already committed them to a Thanksgiving dinner elsewhere, it was secretly fine with me. This meant that not only did I get to cook Christmas dinner that year, but now I got to be in charge for Thanksgiving, too.

The first thing that happened was that Edie threw her neck out, was unable to move her arm, and couldn't get out of bed. This was tragic for two reasons. The first was that she had spent the previous three weeks fighting off various colds and infections and was really looking forward to finally getting out. The second was that she was not bringing her sausage balls.

Edie had first brought sausage balls to Thanksgiving dinner the year before and they were so undeniably delicious being a) made of sausage and b) made of cheese, that we made her bring them back for Christmas that year. In fact they were so delicious that when I told The Boyfriend that Edie had thrown her neck out and was on bed rest, his first response was, "So what are you saying? No sausage balls?"

"I think what you meant to say is that you hope she feels better."

Despite missing the presence of Edie and her husband, Steve, I pressed on with my Thanksgiving dinner plans. Also invited was Sabrina, a college friend and consummate foodie who offered to help out. When she asked what she could bring, I explained a vegetable would be good since I rarely cook them as I'm allergic to most of them.

"Oooohhh," she responded her eyes getting wide, "maybe I'll do brussels sprouts."

Despite having not had a vegetable since Clinton was in

his first term, I remembered enough about them to know that brussels sprouts weren't always a crowd pleaser.

"Do you think you could bring a more mainstream vegetable that more people would like, like broccoli?"

"That doesn't interest me," she sniffed.

"Brussels sprouts!? Are you kidding me?!" The Boyfriend said when he heard. Yes, and no sausage balls, either.

The Boyfriend was getting really into the meal, too, as well as the wine we were going to pair with it. The year before he had made hot toddies, getting so excited that he even bought those fancy glass Irish coffee mugs. This year we thought a Prosecco we had just discovered was the perfect drink with which to begin the evening.

Our guests, however, had other plans. When Sabrina came in carrying her brussels sprouts she sniffed that white wine made her congested and she already had a cold. Next our friend Beth walked in complaining of cramps and insisting that wine only made them worse. No, wine numbs you to all pain, especially cramps. But she wouldn't hear reason. Because of Edie's absence, we were only expecting two more guests, George and his girlfriend, Karen. Karen we knew didn't drink, but on more than one occasion we'd seen George drink an almost entire bottle of scotch on his own. A burly, fiftyish Chicago comic, he had a round face and red nose and a jolly laugh just like Santa, if Santa's workshop was a moonshine distillery. He'd want a drink.

George walked in with disappointing news. "I'm sorry. I just drank way too much last night and I can't. I'm way too hungover."

What do you mean you can't? You're practically an alcoholic!? It was like finding out Santa wasn't real all over again.

Only back then I eventually grew out of toys. I would never grow out of alcohol.

Our vision for everyone sharing a flute of Prosecco as we snacked on cheese and other appetizers was dashed. When we sat down to eat, Sabrina decided she was ready for Prosecco, after we had moved on to the Côtes du Rhône we had painstakingly paired with the turkey. I was inexplicably annoyed by this and despite having an otherwise fine evening, as soon as the last guest left I sat on the couch and burst into tears. In retrospect, I think I was mostly tired. Cooking Thanksgiving dinner for me had become nearly a week's worth of prep. I had an image in my head of what everything was going to look and taste like and I was usually so pleased with the results that it was worth it. But with guests either absent or under the weather, the days of prep culminated in a very underwhelming finish. The one highlight of the evening was that The Boyfriend discovered he liked brussels sprouts, although nothing made up for the lack of sausage balls.

So for Christmas, we had learned our lesson. By that do I mean that we realized not to put so much pressure on ourselves and have such high expectations? Hell, no. By that I mean that I had learned to not allow my guests a choice, but to enjoy things my way.

One Sunday before Christmas, The Boyfriend and I were at the Colorado Wine Company, drinking away our afternoon at a tasting because we don't have children and can. That's when we were introduced to Bugey Cerdon, a wonderful French sparkler with a deep red color. It tasted great and looked even better. We thought it would be the perfect first drink to serve as people arrived.

Over the next couple of weeks, our dinner plans started to come together, as did the guest list. I shared an office with another writer on *The Soup*, a fellow atheist who would watch *Rudolph the Red-Nosed Reindeer* on YouTube with me when we should have been working, because no one in Hollywood has ever evolved past the age of thirteen. The Boyfriend called him my "Office Boyfriend" and after a few drinks could be heard confessing to him, "You're the only man who knows how hard my job is," as if either one of them were such a fucking treat to deal with. Next to my girls, he was one of my closest friends. And he didn't have plans so he was coming, too.

The guest list got a little larger, the menu got a lot so. In addition to the braised lamb shank and mushroom risotto, Lois was bringing a salad with a cranberry dressing, as well as a chocolate pecan pie, and these German lemon sugar cookies she had made as a child. To The Boyfriend's relief, Edie was bringing her sausage balls, as well as a crab dip appetizer. I made a batch of chocolate espresso cookies since I don't eat either pecans or lemons but I cannot live without dessert. Then The Boyfriend and I got the idea to follow the entrée with a port and Stilton pairing. Now, I couldn't have done this with all of my friends. This may come as a shock, but some of my friends find us pretentious. But damn it, it's my Christmas and if I want to spend it with port and Stilton like an English sea captain, what business is it of theirs? Fortunately the girls and Office Boyfriend were game.

Learning nothing from Thanksgiving, I didn't stop at food. First we decided to also do a Yankee Swap. Or White Elephant. Or Gift Exchange. Everyone calls it something different. It's where you pick a present and you don't know what's in it and you might hate it and if no one else wants it, you could be stuck with it. Some people might just call it, "Gifts from my parents." Then I decided to take it one step further: I bought an ornament specially selected for each individual guest and then stuck it next to their place at the table.

And speaking of their place at the table, we had now graduated to place cards. Lois had bought a house and gotten married the previous year and the first time she had us over for dinner, there were place cards in holders at the table. I didn't understand this throwback to days of yore. It seemed overly fussy, even for me, and I just assumed that the place card holders were a wedding gift that she thought it would be rude not to use.

But I didn't realize someone else was forming opinions about the place cards, as well. The next time we had people over for dinner and Lois and her husband were coming, The Boyfriend flew into a panic late in the afternoon.

"But what are we going to do? We need those things! Those things for the seats! Where are we going to get them?"

It turns out he LOVED place cards. He thought it was genius! I later heard him explain it to someone else, "They're key if you want to avoid that comedy of errors that happens every time you tell people that dinner's ready." It was true. No one wants to commit to a seat at the table when dinner is ready. This makes The Boyfriend crazy because he's trying to serve dinner and everyone is standing around like it's duck, duck, goose—oh wait they actually sit in "duck, duck, goose," don't they? Well, then musical chairs or something and while everyone is hovering over the chairs, The Boyfriend's food is getting cold. But if their name is at a seat, they have to sit down.

I actually saw him approach the table at a rather large dinner party recently and say, "What? No place cards?"

There's another reason place cards are perfect, you can sit that shy person next to someone who might draw them out or make sure the two people who don't get along sit far apart. It's social engineering at its most polite, and even better, yet another way to exercise control over the gathering.

Convinced now that we needed them, I set about trying to find something that would work as place cards without having to go to Michaels crafts store on a Saturday afternoon. But what materials did I have on hand, in extreme excess...? I ended up gluing two wine corks side by side, making a slit in the top of one, and then sliding a piece of card stock in it. My Christmas place cards were equally low tech: a pinecone with a name card slid between the scales. Simple. It was the only thing there that was.

I possibly took the decorating a little too far, deciding to match the decorations to the color scheme in each room, right down to the M&M's. Our living room is painted a retro aqua blue with brown accents and I decorated accordingly. I got a silver tabletop tree, that I stuck on the credenza and only decorated with blue and brown ornaments. I hung white garland with blue balls from the window. Blue snowflakes swung down from every shelf on the brown built-in. A garland of blue balls garnished the center beam. And in the candy dish on the table were brown and blue M&M's. I completed the retro sixties look in the room with five-inch figurines of the Peanuts gang Christmas pageant around the silver tree. I thought it was the most amazing room I had ever been in. I couldn't wait for everyone to see it for themselves.

Finally it was Christmas Eve. And here is where we did learn our lesson from Thanksgiving. Your instinct as a host is to be accommodating and offer people a lot of choices. "What can we get you? We have beer, wine, whiskey, tequila, rum, Coke, juice, water—still and sparkling."

That is wrong. Are you hosting because you are a kind and warm individual who likes to invite people into your home? No. You are hosting because you are an exacting control freak who loves food and wine and knows exactly what should be served with what and when. And this is what happens when you give people choices. They ask for something you don't have, like Diet Dr Pepper, and then you feel like a bad host for not having it, not that you would let them pair a Dr Pepper with a mushroom tart.

We didn't give people the choice that night or the opportunity to make excuses that they were hungover or pussies this time. When people walked in the door that night we handed them each a glass and said, "This is what we're starting with." We timed it so perfectly that when Edie and Steve, the first to arrive, walked through the door, it was to the sound of a cork being popped. It was a great way to get everyone to try something they might not have gravitated toward if we had allowed them a choice. Steve is usually a beer guy. But he politely took what was offered and was the first to ask for a second glass. In fact it was such a hit everyone wanted seconds and we soon ran out, as we only had the one bottle. Next thing I knew, the men had set out on foot to the grocery store a few blocks away for more sparkling wine. It was

Mumm, and my local grocery store is so low rent, they actually keep the Mumm locked up, so the men had to find someone with a key in order to buy it, but they brought back two bottles, laughing about the story.

Here's what makes a Specialty Drink special: it gives the guests something in common immediately. Everyone suddenly has a shared experience they can talk about. I know it seems like not that big of a thing. But when I look back at the hot toddies the year previous, everyone had something to say.

"I've never had a hot toddy before, have you?"

"I've never made them with apple cider, we usually use tea."

"I like the cinnamon."

"What fucking pretentious thing do they have us doing now?"

The same thing happened that Christmas with the sparkling wine.

"I normally don't like champagne, but I love this."

"I'm going to go get more."

"I'll go with you."

It's an instant icebreaker, even among people who shouldn't need the ice broken. But the reality is that sometimes you do, even among your best friends, even with your significant other. People lead busy, hectic, stressful lives and when you walk in the door, it's hard to leave all of that background noise behind, even if it's with someone you're really looking forward to seeing. There's always an adjustment period, where you slowly ease into the night and stop thinking about what you did, should have done, have to do. Talking about something you are experiencing in the here and now forces you to be present with each other. And I think that's why I burst into tears that Thanksgiving night: the night felt disjointed because we all brought the background noise in with us, but never found a way to turn it off. A specialty drink can bring a dinner party together.

There were no tears on Christmas Eve, in fact quite the opposite. Everyone had done such a great job cooking that the table was full of inquiries about how things had been prepared, whose recipe they had used, where the ingredients were bought. It was nice to find ourselves surrounded by friends who also took such pleasure in food and wine. It gave me an idea. A week later I sent Lois and Edie an e-mail.

> Given all of this—the dinner, the fun we had cooking, the love we all have of food and finding the perfect recipe, and the great new wine book I gave The Boyfriend—I would like to propose a dinner once a month. We split up courses, find fun new things, pair wines to go with it, and alternate houses to host. Please say, "Yes."

We called ourselves the Girls' Cooking Club, and hosted one dinner a month, always with a lone seventh guest, whom we fondly referred to as "The Interloper." Lois made whole themes out of place cards. The Boyfriend and I paired wines to every course. Edie and I would both do "dress rehearsals" when it was our turn to cook the entrée, so that nothing was left to chance the night of. That inaugural year culminated with the three of us throwing a holiday party for eighty guests. We did everything: we made the appetizers, the desserts, provided red, white, and sparkling wines, as well as beer and a full bar. It was cocktail attire and we bought cheap glassware at Ikea, because we refused to watch anyone drink out of a plastic cup. I dropped thirty-five dollars on a special pan at Williams-Sonoma, just so I could make tiny little mushroom tarts. One thing was certain, I was getting in way too deep.

Tip

As a good hostess you think people want choices. Not true. People are sheep devoid of taste who need to be told what to eat and that they like it. If you hand a guest something, they will most likely feel obligated to try it and even if they don't like it, they will feel a sense of self-importance for having tried something new.

Chapter 8
How to Throw a Baby Shower for 100 People and Not Hate Babies or People

Lois was pregnant.

Not only was she pregnant, she wanted to be. Pregnant.

I myself have never lost the attitude I had toward pregnancy in high school: it was what you absolutely did not want to happen and you worked to prevent it at all costs. When friends actually started becoming pregnant by choice, I didn't know what to make of it. They would call me up, all excited.

"Guess what! I'm pregnant!"

"Oh, no! What are you going to do? Do you need a ride?"

Much as they tried to convince me that not only did they want this baby, but that it was in fact, planned, I was as embarrassed for them as if they were a teen mom. "But you had your whole life ahead of you. And now you've ruined it because of one careless moment."

Lois was my first really good friend to have a baby. I mean, sure, I'd had other good friends who'd had babies, but they were no longer good friends, mostly because they were caught up in bullshit with the kid, at the kid's school or with the kid's sitter. And before you think I'm some cold, heartless friend with less of a maternal instinct than Courtney Love, let me just say that for all of those friends, I threw baby showers. I bought cute outfits. I made fancy desserts and decorated. Sure, I might not be happy about the reason, but I won't turn down an excuse to throw a party.

But now Lois was pregnant. And I was trying hard to convince myself that my life wasn't over. Lois was my partner in fun who decided we were going to London over an idle conversation at Anthropologie. Just the year before we had gone to Italy together with her husband and The Boyfriend. We had spent countless summer afternoons sipping wine at various Southern Californian pools, whether hers, mine, or some hotel's. She was there when all of my mommy friends failed me. Our lives were so fabulous like they were, why bring a baby into it? Our lives were too much fucking fun for a baby!

Telling myself I had to be brave, I smiled and congratulated her. I knew it was what she wanted, no matter how half-baked an idea it might seem to me. I did tell her, however, that her baby was, "the last baby I have room in my heart and my head to care about." Again, before you judge me, let me just say that friends' babies are cute creatures who within a few years grow into children who want nothing to do with you. I'm just ahead of them. And there was just too damn many of them, now. I had tried to be the supportive friend. I give not a whit of a fuck about breast-feeding, vaccinations, or preschools and yet I have sat there listening while people not only droned on about all of these things, but then got mad at you if you so much mentioned another friend doing something different. I have tried to maintain friendships by hanging out with women and their kids when they couldn't find a sitter, only to spend the night with some misbehaved toddler who should have been in bed hours ago, now throwing a tantrum because ... they should have been in bed hours ago. One friend's little girl actually used to stare me down until I left, even if it was one in the morning. What is she doing up at one in the morning!? I really tried. But throughout all of this, I felt my efforts to maintain the friendships weren't always reciprocated, and it seemed that having kids was considered a perfectly fine excuse for the lack of reciprocation. And then they would all ask me when I wanted kids, and I bit my tongue so as not to say, "If having kids means that I have to give up every reward-ing adult relationship that I have, I'm not quite sure that I want them."

> AUTHOR'S NOTE: If you are reading this book and have kids, of course I don't mean you. And thanks for buying the book!

Maybe it's just not feasible for those with kids to be friends with the childless. Maybe we just have to agree to part ways until their youngest goes to college, save those few friends who come in from out of town once a year, sans kids, ready for a good time. (The corollary is also true. When you go to another city, people with kids are usually excited enough to get a sitter for the night and hear what you've been up to.)

Whatever the answer, one thing was certain: I was tired of throwing baby showers, tired of buying baby shower gifts, and really tired of playing baby shower games. But like Leonardo DiCaprio in *Inception*, I had one last caper before I could retire and go back to my old life. One last baby shower until I was out.

Despite what may seem like my piss-poor attitude toward reproduction, I wanted this shower to be wonderful for Lois. She had done a multitude of wonderful things for me over the years, including what I think of as the most selfless thing another person has ever done for me. When we had taken that trip to Italy the year before, The Boyfriend and I flew in four days ahead of her and Clark, her husband, so that we could see Rome. I had already been, but The Boyfriend hadn't and being a huge ancient history buff, there was a lot he wanted to see. The forecast called for rain, but having lived in Southern California for close to ten years, I had forgotten what that meant when I packed. I brought shoes that I would wear in LA in the rain, when I had access to my car and my outdoor walking was fairly limited. I did not bring shoes to wear around a city where all of the ruins are outdoors and it's going to thunder and be cold and there will also be a fair amount of puddles as you schlep around all day.

I spent the first day there buying socks every chance I got and changing the now wet ones out for dry ones. Of course, they didn't stay dry very long. It's a sad day when the only shopping you are doing in Rome is for socks, but I could not buy enough. Because once wet, they stayed that way for the next couple of days, unless I took half an hour to dry them with the small hotel hair dryer. At the end of the second day of this, I had to call Lois and throw myself on her mercy. Would she consider driving forty minutes round trip to my house—the day before she is supposed to leave the country— pick up my rain boots, and somehow find room for them in her suitcase, while trying to pack for herself for two weeks in a foreign country? I knew I was asking a lot but I was desperate. I couldn't get through the next week like this. But Lois agreed like it was no big deal. And for that I will always be indebted to her.

Luckily, I had Edie, dedicated childless friend as well as dedicated party planner, to throw the shower with. We had just thrown a shower for our friend Grace the year before, a traditional all-girls affair. Grace had loved *Alice in Wonderland* since childhood, so we gave it a Mad Hatter Tea Party theme. Being the summer, we served iced tea and lemonade with little sandwiches and some sort of cucumber and yogurt salad that looked good in the magazine, but whose recipe yielded an inadequate amount of yogurt dressing to spread over it, which I learned only when it was too late. An hour before the guests showed up, I was battling a hangover *and* the dressing as I tried to cover the entire dish with it. Fortunately I'm allergic to everything in the salad, so I never had to see if the taste was woefully inadequate, too. Moral of the story: don't make something you've never tried before if you have twenty guests coming over. Also, try not to drink so much the night before you have twenty guests coming over.

Grace's shower was in my backyard and Edie had gone out of her way to blow up *Alice in Wonderland* characters on foam core and place them throughout, including a Cheshire

Cat in the lemon tree. I spent the morning having twenty-five balloons blown up, all depicting various other characters from the book as well: there were flamingos and playing cards and even a lizard that we were going to tie to the chimney on the outdoor fireplace, because somewhere in *Alice in Wonderland,* that happens. Only it was unseasonably windy for Los Angeles in July. The foam core characters kept blowing out of the trees and falling over. The balloons whipped around so much that you couldn't tell what they were supposed to be. And despite the brightly colored centerpieces of various thrift store mugs and teapots with flowers in them, the tablecloths kept blowing up and off the tables. Also, did I mention I was hungover?

Even with the wind and the hangover, the shower was fantastic. Everyone had a good time and we played minimal games. I don't know if you're aware of the concept of baby shower games. As if putting a bunch of women in one room together for an afternoon to discuss all manner of offal like the possibility of episiotomies or your asshole falling out during labor (a phenomenon I have only recently learned existed) weren't enough, you also have to play games. Games with horrible names like "Baby Bingo," where instead of calling out "B2" they call out "baby blanket." Games like "Guess how big around the mom's belly is," which can't be fun for the guests, the mom, or the dad-to-be when he has to hear about it later that night. Games like "Guess the flavor of baby food," and "How quick can you change a diaper," a game that I'm told actually involves fake poop inside of it.

I attended a shower for a very cool friend whose very uncool friends had clearly taken over. During the party, not only did the games never end, but we were required to bring a baby picture of ourselves for the purposes of a particular game, and we were all pinned with a tiny diaper upon our arrival, that was to be unfolded at a later time with some mystery number or something inside of it. I never found out the point of the baby picture or the diaper. I hung out for a while, not knowing anyone; our one friend in common traitorously late, abstaining from the signature cocktail they were serving because it had fruit in it, before quietly ducking out. I was determined to throw a better party (not that the bar was set too high . . .).

Fortunately, Lois wanted no games at her shower. She and her husband wanted the shower to be co-ed, so everyone agreed to forgo games. I was relieved to have no games, but resentful of the double standard. Why not put a man through what every female ages twenty to forty-five is forced to endure every time a condom breaks? Also, Lois had asked to not open gifts at the shower. She made the same request at her bridal shower and I loved her for this. She felt self-conscious opening all of those gifts in front of people, feeling obligated to react to everything and I knew exactly how she felt. I don't like opening one or two gifts in front of people. And I hate it when they make you sit through the hour-long presentation of gifts at other showers. Do you know how hard it is to muster up excitement for that plastic Sophie the Giraffe that's the latest in baby gifts? Especially when I just saw it, going through your registry half an hour before I came here. C'mon, Parents-to-Be. Don't tell me *you're* even this excited for that stuff. You already know what it is, because you asked for it. And is that five pack of replacement breast shields for your breast pump really going to rock your world like a blue box from Tiffany's?

No gifts. No games. Boys. So far Lois's foray into mother-hood was exceeding expectations.

We knew the guest list would be large. Once something is co-ed there's just no way around it. Everyone gets a date, even if it's the person in the office who only started three weeks ago, but that you can't not invite because everyone else in the office is going. With dates, we were looking at close to a hundred people. Even if all of them didn't come, it was still a lot for my house. Plus, Clark worked with a lot of people professionally that The Boyfriend also worked with. And I knew he would drive himself crazy trying to get every last home improvement project done so that no one in a position to hire him had to see the paint peeling off the back patio or that we had turned the back bathroom shower into one big cat box. Needless to say, we were relieved when Lois and Clark offered up their house for the event. This was particularly fortuitous because within a few weeks of ac-cepting their offer, we decided to completely renovate our kitchen.

We had spent nearly three and a half years cooking and throwing dinner parties in a kitchen that not only lacked all function, but was probably poisoning us as well. The cabi-nets were originally from 1947 and had no runners inside the drawers. It was literally wood on wood and each time you pulled a drawer out, it rained sawdust down on the pots and pans below. The paint on the inside was peeling away and I'm pretty sure the only thing holding it all together were the layers of shelf paper lining the otherwise-disgusting insides. There was one drawer that was particularly loathsome, be-ing stained with so much grease and dust that the only thing we thought fit to store in it was the cat litter scooper, and even that was questionable. The backsplash stopped for no reason in the middle of the wall. The tile behind the stove was completely missing in the middle. The floor was this ugly Mexican tile that everything you dropped broke on, even if it was plastic. In an effort to make things somehow more bearable, I had painted the cabinets a light purple to match my KitchenAid and we made the walls yellow to match a Helen Frankenthaler print that we hung in there and the whole effect resembled an Easter egg dying kit gone rogue. But bear in mind, it was still an improvement on what it had looked like when we got there.

Given that we were such entertainers and cooks, we dreamed about being able to redo the kitchen. It always seemed like such an overwhelming project, not to mention expense, so I can't recall what made us think we could do it. However, the housing market had taken a dive so there were a lot of really talented carpenters out of work, and slowly we began to put together a plan that seemed manageable. Only it was mid-April. Lois's shower was the first week in June. And The Boyfriend and I were leaving for Italy ten days after that. I was wary about starting a kitchen renovation a month before we were leaving the country and throwing a baby shower for a hundred people, but The Boyfriend assured me that it was perfect, because he would be off from work the whole time and able to manage things at home and also grill out back at night. So we pulled the trigger on the remodel and he immediately took a new job that lasted almost the entirety of the renovation.

When you work as a staff writer, you want a boss who likes to go home. Get a boss who wants to avoid his family and you will find yourself working until all hours of the night and sometimes, early morning. This explains why The Boyfriend found himself working on Memorial Day, a few weeks into our remodel. Normally our Memorial Days were sunny poolside affairs shared with friends. This one was cold and overcast and I spent it alone, save for the painter who spent the whole time yelling at me that he never would have agreed to work that day if he knew it was Memorial Day, like it was my job to keep his calendar. It was so damp the paint wasn't drying so he asked to borrow my hairdryer, which within minutes became covered with a thick crust of spackle and paint, never to find its way inside my bathroom again. The next day before I went back to work, I carefully explained to the painter how to lock the house up, The Boyfriend already long gone to work. I came home, alone (The Boyfriend was working another late night), to an unlocked house. Inside, the painter had removed the Ram Board that separated the kitchen remodel from the rest of the house, leaving a can of paint open in the middle of it, where my cats (We had three now. Shut up.) were free to roam around, get paint on their paws, track it all around the new kitchen before licking it off of themselves, giving themselves some form of paint poisoning. Also, we hadn't grilled the entire time. I had had enough.

Given all of that, when we tried to figure out how to feed one hundred people at a baby shower, cooking wasn't an option. Fortunately, we found out Lois was having a boy and a plan came together. We would make the theme of the shower, "Boy." We would serve hot dogs and Oreo cookies with milk and have a keg. We would set up a Wii or an Xbox or whatever the thing is that guys waste their time with when they

could be telling me how much they love me. I located a cater-
ing company that could send a New York–style hot dog cart
to the house. They would bring everything with them and
take it all away when they left. For a girl without a kitchen,
about to go to Europe, this was perfect.

Once we came up with the "Boy" theme, everything fell
into place. We would do minimal decorations, not wanting to spoil Lois's perfectly appointed midcentury modern
home, or cart another twenty-five helium balloons around. I
bought a bunch of "boy toys" at the 99¢ Only Store—cars
and helicopters and squirt guns—and placed them around
the food and gift table as accents. When we were done with
the party, it all went to Goodwill. In addition to the beer, we
bought red, white, and sparkling wine and luckily still had
all of those Ikea glasses left over from the Christmas party
Lois, Edie, and I had thrown the year before.

I'm not going to lie. There was a certain amount of pressure for this party. None that I felt from Lois or Clark, but
that I was putting on myself. In addition to wanting to give
them a special event that would live up to our already high
standards, this was Hollywood. The guest list included people who were executives or millionaires or on TV shows,
who are used to parties that are being professionally catered
and thrown by party planners. I was a TV writer with no
kitchen who was leaving for Italy in a week. The party had to
be low maintenance and yet also be the best party any of
these people had ever attended or ever would in their lives. I
had now put myself in a situation where I had to find a way
to impress a group of people I already struggled most days
to impress professionally. Only this time, I had to impress

them with my skills in an area that is not even my actual profession, but that somehow I take almost as seriously. I made a mental note to buy more wine. I was going to need it.

In addition to the hot dogs, we thought it would be fun to serve grilled-cheese sandwiches for people who don't eat meat or whatever is in a hot dog. We looked into a couple of services similar to the hot dog cart that did grilled cheeses, but the expense seemed excessive for what we were getting. I couldn't let go of the idea, but we were running out of options and it looked like it wasn't going to happen.

That's when Edie suggested that we just do it ourselves. Not actually make everyone a grilled cheese. But that we would set up a grilled cheese bar of breads, a selection of cheeses, toppings like tomatoes, bacon, walnuts, and honey. We'd have two panini makers on at all times and let people design their own grilled cheese. We had already planned to have two "helpers" on hand, i.e., friends who were actors, who we paid for the afternoon to just make sure people had drinks and that the trash didn't pile up. One could also linger by the grilled-cheese station to help people cook their sandwich.

Finally the day of the shower came. At my house, the newly fabricated countertops had been placed on top of the custom-built, not gross inside, cabinets making the kitchen almost functional. Italy was a little over a week away. We all arrived early to set up at Lois and Clark's. Edie's husband and The Boyfriend were hooking up the Wii as Edie set up the grilled-cheese station, Clark pumped the keg and I was chilling the wine. That's when Maggie showed up with six pallets of beverages.

Maggie was a mutual friend of all of ours who had

wanted to help out. Only the problem was she told everyone but me that she wanted to help. I don't want to sound ungrateful. Her heart was in the right place. But if you want to help, you can start by contacting me. If I have to pick up the phone and call you, that's not really helping me. That's creating more work for me. Maybe I was being testy, but I was also in the middle of a kitchen remodel and about to leave the country.

Conversely, Katie, another friend also wanted to help. She e-mailed me. She thanked me for putting the shower together and asked if she could do anything to help. When I stepped back and realized that all of the food was going to consist of carbs, cheese, and unidentified pork products, I asked her to bring a veggie plate or two. Done and done.

Eventually Maggie contacted me or maybe I just got sick of hearing people tell me to call her or even more likely I had Edie do it. Like I said, I was a little on edge. My fridge was in the living room and I made coffee in my bathroom every morning. In any event, we asked Maggie to bring some non-alcoholic beverages for guests. Maybe some water bottles, and a few two-liter bottles of soda. At least that's the picture Edie and I had in our minds, having thrown parties before and knowing what gets drunk and what doesn't. In my tense state of mind, I completely overlooked that Maggie may not have thrown as many parties, and certainly for not as many people, because this is what showed up at Lois's house that morning.

70 bottles of water
24 bottles of Snapple—3 kinds
35 cans of Coke

48 bottles Hansen's soda—4 kinds
35 cans of Coke Zero
35 cans of Diet Dr Pepper
40 Capri Sun juice bags

We had almost three hundred beverages for not quite a hundred people and that was not including the wine and beer! Never mind that we were never going to drink it, we had no place to put it, and could barely carry it all into the house!

Luckily, there was also plenty of sparkling wine, a perfectly acceptable beverage to drink before noon and before your guests arrive.

And soon enough they did. Despite being forced to come to a shower, the menfolk seemed quite content with the keg, hot dogs, and Wii bowling. As we had promised, there were no games, except for the Wii and this brainchild of Edie's that we had done for Grace's shower. She scanned ten baby pictures of Lois and Clark, printing each of them on the top of the page with the instructions that we were to caption them. Because so many of the guests were comedy writers, the pressure was on. It was a fun thing for guests to do, too, because it gave them something to distract themselves with if they didn't know anyone there, without forcing people to interact with strangers and guess the circumference of Lois's stomach. None of the women seemed to miss the games or seemed to mind that we weren't opening gifts and appeared quite happy to enjoy the sunny day on the lanai with a glass of wine in their hand. I even saw a few of them eating hot dogs.

But the real surprise was the grilled-cheese station. Halfway through the shower we ran out of everything. This seemed completely inconceivable to us just days before when we were buying pounds of cheese and at least half a dozen loaves of bread. Nobody eats carbs in LA! But that day they did. Realizing the shower was going to last at least another hour and a half, we sent Edie's husband out on an emergency run to the grocery store for more of everything.

Perhaps most importantly was that we were all relaxed, the presence of our actor-helper-friends greatly reducing the stress levels for all of us. Not only were Lois and Clark able to enjoy their friends, but Edie and I spent an anxiety-free afternoon, talking to friends, too. And when the final guests left, we all poured another cocktail, took off our heels, and gathered around the baby photos to read the captions out loud to each other laughing hysterically. Given the talent in the house that day, there were some wickedly funny quotes.

A month after their son was born, Lois and Clark were out at my birthday party, the baby with a sitter, our friendship resuming its normal course in a lot less time than it took any of us to give away those forty-eight bottles of Hansen's soda.

Tip

If you really want to help a host or hostess out, don't say, "Call me if you need something." They don't have time to call you. They don't have time to throw this elaborate party they've committed to. Instead, call, or even better, e-mail them and offer a few suggestions as to what might be helpful that you can do. Love to make dip? Offer to do that! Can't cook but drive a car? Ask them if they need anything picked up. This way you're not putting the ball back in their overcommitted court.

Recipe
How to Set Up a Bar for 100 People and Not Have 74 Bottles of Snapple Left Over

Ingredients
Alcohol

No one wants to run out of alcohol at a party, and yet trying to estimate how much to buy can be confusing. The first thing to do is to limit your options. Have one kind of red and one kind of white. Buy one kind of beer. If you're going to serve hard alcohol, limit it to one or two. Ask yourself if your friends who like mixed drinks tend to prefer vodka or are they rum drinkers? Think about the seasons. People seem to prefer rum and tequila in warmer months and vodka and whiskey in the winter. What's the type of party? If you're having a pool party, are people going to want a margarita, or a single malt scotch, no ice?

The same holds true for nonalcoholic beverages. You don't need seven kinds of soda. In fact, I would limit it to one. Decide whether or not the majority of your friends are diet or regular, Coke, Pepsi, or Sprite and then buy that. Let what would be a good mixer be your guide. If you want to have a juice option, both as a mixer and for your nondrinking friends, then you may want to go with OJ over cranberry juice, unless you think your nondrinking friends are also all suffering from urinary tract infections. Maybe you don't want to do soda or juice, but you make a mean homemade ice tea or lemonade. Whatever you decide to serve, just keep it simple. You are entertaining people for a few hours. They are not marathon runners who are dangerously dehydrated. If the people who aren't drinking alcohol would like a beverage the one or two options you have should be just fine.

Always have water. Everyone likes to drink it. Your drunks need it and your sober people might prefer it to soda. You can decide for yourself if you want small bottles, big jugs, or a pitcher straight from your tap. Do whatever is easy for you. If you don't want to keep refilling a pitcher, buy small bottles. If you don't want to spend the money or want to leave less of a carbon footprint, put a couple of pitchers out in advance, or always keep a backup chilling in the fridge.

So how much should you buy? When it comes to soft drinks, I wouldn't get individual cans, I would just get a two-liter bottle, one per four or five people I think *are not* drinking booze. Same thing with juice. If you want to buy individual water, buy one bottle per guest. Some people may have two or three, some will have none and the worst thing that happens is that you have leftover water.

Now my math is not perfect. If I was that great at math, I wouldn't have bought a house at the height of the market. These are guidelines that seem to work for my friends. They may be bigger drunks than your friends. Or perhaps your friends are some hedonistic strain of barbarians that would put rock stars to shame. I estimate one bottle of wine per two guests. Again, some people won't have any, some will take the whole bottle and ask what you're going to have. With beer I would go with two guests per six-pack assuming the same thing. When it comes to hard liquor, I've rarely seen anyone need more than one bottle of whatever it is you're serving.

Remember, people will usually bring alcohol, too. So if fifteen bottles of wine seems excessive for thirty guests, get ten knowing that people will probably bring you a couple of bottles. Maybe your friends aren't wine drinkers. Maybe they prefer beer. Try to adjust accordingly. Most importantly keep in mind these two things:

1. There are worse things in life than having leftover alcohol.
2. If you run out of anything, it's probably time for them to go.

Lastly, don't forget the ice. If you're like us and you've never hooked up your ice maker because you never need a beverage to be that cold, then don't forget to pick up a bag, two if it's hot out.

Chapter 9
How to Carry a Theme Too Far

The rest of the summer following Lois's shower was peaceful and drama free. So I figured why not fuck all that up?

Less than four weeks after we started the renovation, we were moving our things back into the kitchen. We then almost immediately got onto a red-eye for Italy, so that the first person to truly enjoy cooking in our new kitchen was in fact, our house sitter. Nonetheless, we returned at the end of June, just in time to celebrate the Fourth of July, a rather low-key affair, at least for me. Dinner parties inside the house mean food cooked inside the house as well. That means making sure we have a set of plates that aren't chipped, glasses that aren't broken, and place cards. It means I make the table pretty with candles and flowers and lintbrush the placemats as they are one of my cat's favorite place to nap and lick her privates. Dinner outside means dinner cooked outside and that is The Boyfriend's domain.

When we started looking for houses, I secretly wanted a pool. I say "secretly" because I was trying to not draw too much attention to the fact that I *desperately* wanted a pool. The Boyfriend was having a hard enough time coming to terms with buying a house. I didn't want to scare him off entirely. But about two or three years before, this East Coast girl had come to terms with living in LA thanks to three things: tennis, convertibles, and pools.

I had a terrible time adjusting to the lifestyle of LA. I hated driving. I missed my old neighborhoods in Boston where I could walk as I ran my errands, getting lost in the architecture and sights. And then I got a convertible. It's a much different experience when you drive around LA with the top down, staring up at palm trees as you go. In the winter, I would turn the heat on, just so I wouldn't have to put the top up. Around the same time I made a friend who had a pool. When we stopped hanging out, I realized that the thing I would miss the most was her pool. And so I vowed to get my own house with my own pool. Problem solved.

But first I had to sell The Boyfriend on the pool. Being Southern California, pools were almost as abundant as nose jobs and less expensive. Plenty of houses in our price range had pools, and every time the realtor would mention that a house had one, I would try to sound casual as I said, "That sounds nice."

"We don't need a pool," admonished The Boyfriend.

I remind him of this as we are floating on a Sunday afternoon, reading, and enjoying a dry rosé.

"Oh, no, you have to have a pool," he said as he floated by.

Our lives move outdoors in the summertime. The pool was open for anyone and everyone who wanted to stop by.

We grilled. We drank. We lay in the sun and made each other laugh. Also, we had a tiki bar. Our first summer in the house George, our aforementioned scotch-drinking, Santa Claus–looking comic friend, set up shop there. He sat on the stool behind the bar and never left, smoking cigarettes and making everyone else laugh. In between, he took it upon himself to make his own signature cocktail, a mix of various fruit punches, pineapple sodas, and rum that I never had the pleasure of tasting due to my allergies, but everyone else seemed to really enjoy. At the end of our first summer we had a party and one guest said we should always hire that bartender for our events. Guests delighted in sitting near him, listening to his stories as he poured them drinks. In the end, George was always still standing; however, many of our guests weren't as lucky.

And that's how our summer weekends went. We never made plans during the day because we wanted no excuse not to be in our backyard. And we rarely made plans at night, because we didn't want to have to rush off and were resentful when we did. But then I got another one of my bright ideas.

I swear, if I go too long without planning something an alarm goes off in me. All of a sudden I'm the Manchurian Candidate of entertaining. I have this mysterious instinct to just start making plans. Out of nowhere I get this party imperative.

"Hey, you know who we haven't seen in a while . . . ?"

"You know what would be fun?"

"I was thinking we could . . ."

For example, one of my friends in LA just so happens to have been friends with the wife of one of the writers on my show—twenty years ago. They found each other on Facebook and then found they had me in common, and in all honestly probably could have both left it that way for another twenty years had I not decided that this was an excuse for all of us to get together. Most people don't set up playdates for the wives of their co-workers and men they knew in the nineties. I can't help it. It's a compulsion. It's like I'm Russell Crowe in *A Beautiful Mind,* only the patterns I see when I look at my calendar are connections between people and events and themes.

And that's exactly what happened as I started looking forward to the premiere of the new season of *Mad Men.* We loved the show and a lot of our friends did, too. And rather than just be content to discuss it at work the next morning, I thought it would be fun to host a cocktail party celebrating the premiere, and people could dress in vintage garb and maybe we'd have some 1960s cocktail weenies.

Despite the fact that neither The Boyfriend nor I has much of a taste for hard liquor, we decided we should serve martinis. Never mind that neither one of us knew how to make one or that the only time I ever drank martinis was when chocolate ones were popular in 1999. Yes, I was that girl.

Having never actually had a martini, we wanted to experience them the way they were originally made, which meant gin and vermouth. Now we had always made fun of gin. It seemed like the type of liquor drunk by old men at the local VFW hall. Gin being your preferred liquor seemed like the result of a lot of bad choices in life. Whenever gin was brought up, we always had a laugh reminding ourselves of the story we had heard from a friend who, through a series of events, found himself required to attend a weekend detox. One old guy there opened up by saying, "I love the taste of gin in the morning." That was what we associated with gin drinkers. If you drank gin, odds are your kids didn't talk to you and they referred to your wife's second husband as their dad.

Still, I had friends who were dedicated martini drinkers who insisted that there was only one kind of martini and anything else was a vodka drink. And certainly I was confused, not only by the people drinking vodka martinis, but by those same people who didn't even use vermouth. Not to be all type A and a stickler for detail, but isn't that just vodka straight up?

So we wanted to be authentic. And as luck would have it, we found ourselves the week before the party, enjoying another wine tasting at our local wine and spirits store. You couldn't really refer to Flask Fine Wines as a "liquor store;" it was carpeted and there were no lottery tickets being sold. And instead of finding behind the cash register someone who couldn't hack the pressure of Target or who had assumed a new identity and was laying low for a while, you had actual experts on the wine and spirits you were purchasing. (Although I don't doubt that the liquor store employee who owes six months of child support is an expert on the subtle differences between Jägermeister and lamp oil.)

Ray was one of the owners of Flask Fine Wines and a veteran of the restaurant business. When he spoke it was with an authority and certainty that made me want to listen to him implicitly whether it was on which Napa Cab to buy or when to send a handwritten thank you note. So it was no surprise that he not only would know exactly how to make a martini, but that we would follow his instructions.

He recommended a gin and showed us to the vermouth and told us how many parts of each he would mix when he was tending bar. And then he explained that in the early sixties, they didn't actually use shakers. The hosts would make martinis in a pitcher—stirred—and then pour them into a chilled glass. Of course they did! Why else would James Bond have needed to say, "Shaken, not stirred?" Unfortunately, the store didn't sell pitchers, but they did toss in a shaker leftover from a promotion into our bag on the way out.

There are two types of people who get invited to theme dress-up parties. The people who turn to their significant others and say, "Are you fucking kidding me?" and the people who have been waiting all of their lives for such an occasion because they bought just the thing to wear years ago in case the opportunity should ever arrive. I am one of the latter. I still have a vintage dress with a gorgeous, white pleated chiffon skirt and purple velvet bodice that I look like an ice skater in and that I have yet to find the right place to wear it. I bought it nine years ago. But when the opportunity does arrive, I will be ready.

Throughout the week, I started finding out which of the two categories my friends were in.

Edie's e-mail immediately asked if it was, "fifties cocktail or fifties bridge game?" Whereas another friend basically said that her contribution to the theme dress would be that she would be smoking. In between assuaging people that, "No, of course, they didn't have to dress up," or hearing about how plaid was very fifties to explain why they would be wearing a flannel shirt, Edie was hard at work researching fifties style appetizers and Heather immediately said she was bringing something called a "flaming weenie tree."

All week long when we talked about running out to get things, The Boyfriend would say, "Don't forget we need to get a pitcher." So when I found myself up early the Sunday morning of the party, I used the opportunity to pick up the last-minute things that we needed, one of which was a glass pitcher. I had been in a bad mood the day before and I wanted to do something nice for him. I thought The Boyfriend would be pleased when I got home and all of the errands for the day were done, the pitcher he couldn't stop talking about purchased. And he was. "Thanks," he said when he saw it, "that's great."

Which only made what happened next so curious.

Heather and her husband, Robert (not Dick), arrived first, needing some time to assemble the flaming weenie tree. Turns out it was a head of purple cabbage with skewers stuck into it and carved out on the top to allow for a can of Sterno. Cocktail weenies were then stuck on the skewers and the Sterno was lit, providing you a decorative place to now feast your weenies. Voilà! Flaming weenie tree.

As our first guests had arrived, I decided it was time to make the martinis, which I did, in the pitcher, per the instructions I had received. Then The Boyfriend came in, looked at the pitcher and said, "What are you doing? I'm going to make them in the shaker."

Robert had just walked in a moment before and was standing behind us as I said, "Well then why the hell did you want me to get a pitcher?!" He didn't really have an explanation. He just said, "Robert wants a martini. I'm going to make him one." Robert was Southern and thus well-mannered and clearly at a loss as to whether it would be more polite to stay and act as if nothing had happened or to just leave as if he were never there. I quickly solved the problem for him. "Do you want a martini, Robert? The Boyfriend can make you one or you could have one of my shitty martinis," before turning on my heels and leaving in a huff, making sure I poured myself a healthy glass of my "shitty pitcher martini" on the way out. SIDE NOTE: gin's not so bad.

Common sense said that I should have just let The Boyfriend do what he wanted, as my part in the party had been completed so I could just sit back and enjoy drinking with my friends, which was really what this was all about. That's what common sense said. But common sense also said that you would not tell your girlfriend for a solid week straight that you needed a pitcher for martinis if—when she made martinis in said pitcher—you were just going to look at her like she had wiped cat poop across her forehead, ask her what she was doing, and tell her you wanted to use a shaker. No, common sense was clearly not on the guest list for this soirée.

I went out to the patio and told Heather what had happened, who no doubt told me to let it go. Then Edie and Steve arrived. I asked Steve if he wanted one of my shitty martinis. He looked confused, but I was only too happy to fill him in. In response, he mumbled something about not really liking gin. I, however, was surprised to find that it didn't taste nearly as horrible as I thought it did, but maybe that was the vermouth. Despite the alcohol's effects on my taste buds, it was having zero effect on my personality. It wasn't making me angrier, luckily, although I'm not sure that was even possible. But it wasn't mellowing me out about the pitcher, either. This was evidenced by the fact that when The Boyfriend walked out a few minutes later, I immediately went back inside. I wasn't ready to play nice.

I have always prided myself on the fact that no matter what our other faults are as a couple, we don't fight in front of other people. Ever. But that night I couldn't help myself. Edie was in the kitchen preparing her fifties hors d'oeuvres, a saltine cracker spread with melted butter and cayenne pepper that was surprisingly delicious, and I took turns helping her and complaining about the pitcher all over again. Lois and Clark arrived and we took a very *Mad Men*–era photo of Lois, nine months pregnant, holding a martini glass as I made Clark sit through the whole offer of the "shitty pitcher martini," which had become my official shtick of the evening. Clark wasted no time taking matters into his own hand, and opted to make himself his own *vodka* martini. So much for the thirty dollars worth of gin that was sitting in the brand-new pitcher AS PER INSTRUCTIONS!

I was being insufferable. I knew it. But I couldn't let it go. Why? The Boyfriend had done entirely ridiculous things and completely contradicted himself before. What was so different about this time? I think in the moment that he said, "What are you doing that for?" I felt dismissed. I was trying to do something that would make him happy. I wasn't the one who wanted the pitcher. If I remember correctly, I wasn't even the one that really wanted to do the martinis. I was trying to do what he wanted and I was dismayed to find that my efforts to give him what he wanted were not actually what he wanted. At a party celebrating the era that created the resentful housewife and the combative couple, I transformed myself for the night into an homage that went deeper than my costume.

We worked it out the old-fashioned way, too: he bought my forgiveness. Flowers arrived the next day at the office. Years of trying to resolve disagreements in a healthy way brought us to the compromise that as long as he sends flowers, I can't be mad. (Although one time it took three days of flowers.)

Tip

When it comes to alcohol, most people don't care if it's shaken, stirred, or run over by a truck so long as it gets them good and drunk. But if you have a fight with your boyfriend over how to make a martini, you will be the one feeling shaken, stirred, and run over by a truck the next day. Try to remember that everyone will have a good time as long as the alcohol flows, and put all disagreements on ice.

1) Weenie

2) Flame

3) Cabbage

Flaming Weenie Tree

Chapter 10
How to Learn to Love Yourself Again After Serving Runny Polenta

I had good intentions.

They say the road to hell is paved with good intentions. In my case, the streets were spackled together with runny polenta. Which really doesn't make for a good spackle at all when you consider the whole "runny" thing.

Maybe I should start at the beginning.

My lawyer and The Boyfriend's agent are identical twin brothers. And let me just say here that twins should come with a warning. When you meet one half of a twin (or perhaps a third of a triplet) they should work into conversation almost immediately that they have a twin.

It's the corollary to the rule that when you have a boyfriend, and a guy starts talking to you, you have to find a way to quickly mention your boyfriend in a way that doesn't embarrass either one of you. You can't be all forthright the minute he starts talking and just blurt out, "I have a boyfriend," because it makes you look like you're full of yourself and it makes him feel really transparent and then he has to do something silly to save face like say, "What? You're not all that. I'm not even attracted to you. And I have a girlfriend. Two. Besides, can't a guy just talk to a girl because he wants to be friends?" (No. No guy is ever looking for a new female friend in a bar or most other places.)

You have to be subtle, but still work it in quickly so you don't lead him on. When he asks what you're doing this weekend, and you tell him you're playing tennis, and he feigns interest in that and asks how you like it you say, "My boyfriend and I have been playing mixed doubles for the last two years." Mission accomplished. He can gracefully extract himself and you don't have to spend the night feeling guilty that this guy keeps sporting rounds not knowing that you're drinking the wine that's seventeen dollars a glass.

It's the *exact* same thing with twins.

You should always tell people up front that you have one.

. . . And if he happens to live in the exact same city as you and work in the same industry, that goes double. (No pun intended.)

Romulus did not tell me he had a twin. He was an agent who I knew socially and one afternoon a good year or two into our acquaintance he walked into a party and I said, "Hi," and proceeded to talk to him for a solid five minutes.

And then he walked in again.

I have a vague recollection of saying something stupid like, "Do you have a brother?" at which point I'm introduced to Remus, who is actually the one I've been talking to for the last five minutes, so we've already sort of met.

I am beyond embarrassed. I immediately start apologizing profusely. "I'm sorry, I just thought he was you," which now I realize they must hear a lot. They must hear it so much, in fact, that they didn't have the energy to say, "Of course you did. We're IDENTICAL TWINS!" Because at this point, I don't realize they're identical twins. I don't think they're fraternal twins. I think they're just brothers who look a lot alike and that I've just done something really stupid that everyone is going to hold up as proof that I drink too much when the intervention comes.

(By the way, I also once had a manager who is one third of triplets. I knew this early on. Now, I am prepared. I have no idea what it is about me that attracts multiples, however, it's definitely another reason I am hesitant to attempt procreation.)

Beyond looks, they are identical in one other area: they are really fucking good at making a deal. I'm convinced there was a third brother in the womb who didn't stand a chance against either one of them, and they just divvied him up until there was nothing left. The Boyfriend and I wanted to thank them for their triplet absorbing negotiation skills. We'd thought to take them out to dinner, but with agents and lawyers it's too hard to beat them to the check. But there'd be no check to fight over if we cooked for them at our house.

Joining us for dinner were Romulus's fiancée, a former Miss Albania, and Remus's wife, Carolina, a Southern beauty. Both women have a lot of personality and are a lot of fun, which is not always the case when dealing with wives at the obligatory professional dinner. Sometimes it feels like a full cardio workout just keeping the conversation going until the entrée comes. "What did you study? Where did you go to school? That's a very good school, isn't it? What was Virginia like? How 'fine' was it? Like, you didn't like it 'fine?' Or like you are incapable of thinking of another adjective that could possibly keep this conversation going for longer than ten seconds at a time 'fine?'"

Other times the obligatory professional wives have a lot to say—usually about their husband, their kids, the career they wanted but gave up for them, how their baby is in the lowest percentile for weight but top for height, how expensive their private school is, what work they've had done, what work they would like to have done, how fat they are and how much their size 2 jeans cost.

But Carolina and Miss Albania weren't like that. Carolina had all the gentility of a traditional Southern woman but with a pleasant "no bullshit" chaser. When I e-mailed to find out if there was anything they didn't eat, she immediately wrote back, "We eat everything."

Now I had heard that her husband was picky, but I could see where her Southern manners combined with a certain matter of fact, "You will eat what's on your plate," would never allow her to say that.

Miss Albania's twin was a picky eater, but instead of tough love, she employed treachery. Often she would tell me stories of how she'd liquefy onions in the food processor to give dinner some taste without letting on to him that there was something other than meat and potatoes in it. There was a certain former Eastern Bloc, covert-spy-operation feel to it, and in my head I pictured her wearing a couture trench coat and dark Chanel sunglasses as she smuggled flavor into their meals.

Between being an irrepressible show-off when it comes to dinner parties, and always enjoying the company of both women, I was looking forward to the night a lot.

The day came. I decided to go with a whole Tuscan theme. Carolina and Remus had been to Italy on their honeymoon and Miss Albania had lived there so it was a subject we had all discussed many times. I was making short rib ragu—a favorite of ours that takes two days—and serving it over polenta. The day before I had braised the short ribs, taken all of the meat off the bone, and scraped off the fat and was now reducing it to a ragu. I had set the table with a centerpiece of sunflowers, and decanted a good Italian wine. We laid out a plate of cheeses and truffle honey (Tuscan) and salami (Tuscan). We had bought good scotch (not Tuscan).

Everyone arrived. The men went into the living room and poured scotch. The women drank wine in the kitchen, engaged in our favorite game, "What the men did that afternoon to piss us off." It was going so well. I was babysitting the polenta since I was trying a new technique for cooking it.

A word about polenta: it's the easiest thing in the world that everyone makes a big production over how to cook. One the one hand, I'm not sure why. Water boils, you add polenta, maybe some butter or olive oil, within ten or fifteen minutes it's absorbed all the water and it's more or less finished. Granted, it's hard to keep it the right consistency and it starts to congeal almost immediately upon cooling and pages upon pages are written about how someone can never quite get it like they had in Italy or whatever Mario Batali restaurant took their money last weekend. So while my polenta has always been fine, I thought I could make it better. I wanted it flawless. I had gone from making this night about doing something nice for them, to turning this into the night I could do no wrong for them. I didn't want to allow for the possibility that they had had better polenta in some remote Tuscan village cooked by some know-it-all, show-off nana. They were going to taste my gratitude in every bite, goddamn it. And so I scanned my cookbooks and the Internet and settled on a technique where I had to keep a separate pot of water boiling, periodically adding only the boiling water to the cooking polenta.

> **TIP: Sometimes you have to know when "good enough" will do. This was one of those times.**

Here was my error. The Boyfriend was cooking asparagus as our designated "vegetable." In retrospect, we should have done a salad. A salad is pretty easy to prep earlier in the day. You make your vinaigrette and clean your greens and at the last minute all you have to do is toss it together and serve it on salad plates. This also allows you to serve your braised meats in a shallow bowl, which is perfect because you'll have all those wonderful braising juices that will slowly flood everything else if you serve it on a plate, but that sit just right in a shallow bowl.

Preparing asparagus, however, requires that you cook it right before you serve it unless you want some soggy, overcooked mess. The Boyfriend does his really simply: some garlic, lemon, and olive oil, and maybe about three minutes in the pan, if that. He likes it crisp.

When the polenta was almost ready, I went to tell The Boyfriend that it was go time for the asparagus. I thought to cook it myself, but he's picky about his asparagus and having not eaten a vegetable myself since high school, I thought I should let him do it.

The first thing I saw when entering the living room was the slideshow of our trip to Ireland on the Apple TV. He was showing them vacation pictures! How did this happen!? The amazing dinner party I had prepped for two days to be the envy of all of my friends was going down in flames! We were going to be stigmatized forever as the "people who show vacation slideshows during their dinner parties!"

Now, I want to say here that The Boyfriend is a very gifted photographer who takes hundreds of pictures from all of our trips that we still delight in looking at a couple of times a month. And we have friends as equally into travel and photography as we are, who invite us to look at photos of Italy or Thailand or Africa, and we go happily. However, I recognize that not everyone is as into these things and that some people would rather be invited to the home of the fat couple who swings before they sit through a slideshow of vacation videos, even if it's through the magic of a Steve Jobs–created gadget.

If you looked closely enough, both Romulus and Remus had red in their hair and could trace their ancestry back to the *Mayflower*, and so when the subject of Ireland came up they expressed interest in seeing photos, wanting to go there someday themselves. So I am told. But how many photos? And for how long? This is what I'm thinking as The Boyfriend turns the remote over to me and exits to the kitchen to attend to the asparagus. Now *I'm* the culprit responsible for holding our guests hostage while I try to figure out how much information they want about the ring forts of the Aran Islands. I don't know how fast or slow to go and I can hear myself saying very unwitty and very uncocktail-banter-like things such as, "You know, they prefer to say they speak Irish now because Gaelic to them is an offensive term. . . ." while my brain tries frantically to find a way to pull out of this social nosedive.

Somewhere in all of this it dawns on me that The Boyfriend faced the same dilemma, which is why he insisted on cooking the asparagus. Which he soon announces is done and he starts plating the food for me to carry in.

Only something is not right.

On the plate is a lump of polenta surrounded by a ring of its own water, which is slowly oozing out to the rest of the plate. Instead of placing the ragu over the polenta, he's sort of placed them next to each other, so that their juices are seeping out into each other and the rest of the plate, making for one big watery mess. There are also four stalks of asparagus lying across the plate, like an ineffectual beaver dam.

At this point, I find myself missing my old congealed polenta.

It's my fault. "Why didn't I go back in there?" I ask myself as I am forced to carry the offending polenta to the table. "I should have been there to make sure that everything was still as ready as it had been when I left it. I wasn't there to place it on the plate." There is nothing I can do. I can't save this. It's already on the plate, the table. People are sitting. I can't snatch their plates back and somehow dump everything back in the pot for a do-over. And even if I could, I don't know what I could do over. Except to have been there. "I should have been there to make sure the culmination of two days' worth of cooking looked like something someone had actually spent two days cooking. I should have been there to make sure that the vacation slideshow wasn't going to be the highlight of the night!"

This was my showpiece, my headlining act.

It was ugly.

Who would want to eat this?

These are all of the thoughts going through my head as I try to smile and carry on dinner conversation when all I want to do is run into the bedroom and cry. I want to explain, "I'm a better cook than this! This is not supposed to look like this! I can do better!" But I'm afraid to draw too much attention to what's wrong with it and besides, Julia Child says you should never apologize.

But she doesn't say how you're supposed to let your guests know, "I know it shouldn't be like this," either. In lieu of them thinking I'm this amazing hostess and cook, I want them to at least know that I know what good food is. I don't want us to be that couple that comes up periodically in the social rotation that you dread. "Oh, looks like we have to do another dinner at the Raffertys'. Wonder which thousand pictures of churches they'll show us before they serve us some runny meat on a plate."

And then Remus, in an upbeat voice that clearly means he's drank too much scotch to realize the disaster that sits on the plate in front of him, remarks to Carolina, "Look, honey, grits. You must be so excited."

Polenta is the same thing as the Southern specialty, grits. It's just cooked cornmeal with cheese or butter or oil. And as Carolina kindly says how much she loves grits, my situation, which only a moment ago was dire, reaches a new level of awfulness. I am serving runny grits to a Southern girl. I am serving my runny, ugly, shitty, newfangled awful grits to a Southern girl.

Pass the wine.

By the time Remus and Carolina leave I am temporarily over the runny polenta. In fact, I am so sufficiently buzzed on Italian wine that as I watch Romulus say good-bye to Remus by giving him shit about his gut—or maybe Remus was saying it to Romulus—at this point in the evening I'm afraid of calling them by the wrong name and even though one has shown up with a beard, I can't remember which one that was! I had some other things on my mind, like my crappy polenta and my boring vacation photos! But I have momentarily forgotten that because I am so buzzed, I am afraid the only thought going through my head at the moment is going to escape my lips. Because the only thing I can think looking at the two of them is, "Dude. You two shared the same womb. At the same time. Like wombmates. That's so crazy!"

Out comes the port.

We are snacking on chocolate-covered almonds and espresso beans that I have put out in lieu of dessert. Each place setting has a tiny gift bag filled with candy that doubles as both dessert and place cards as I have written everyone's name on the bag. (God, I was so clever this afternoon! It was all going so well. What happened?) I figured we could seamlessly transition from dinner to something sweet that way, and it's working. High on sugar, alcohol, and caffeine, Miss Albania and I stand in the kitchen till the wee hours talking about her upcoming wedding, psychics, and Montenegro; anything but the runny polenta.

The next day I wake up with the vague notion that I did

something regrettable the night before—which is not en-tirely uncommon. I lay in bed letting my mind play Nancy Drew and solve the Mystery of the Forgotten Regret. Fight with boyfriend? I look next to me. He's there thus he didn't spend the night on the couch . . . so, no, it wasn't that. Then it all comes back to me; I have a Runny Polenta Hangover. It's like a real hangover, except instead of wishing you hadn't drank all of that alcohol, you wish you hadn't served crappy grits to a Southern woman, her husband, his identical twin, and a former Miss Albania.

Speaking of Miss Albania, considering how she and I fin-ished the evening, I'm lucky that a Runny Polenta Hangover is all I have.

However, an alcohol hangover doesn't last as long and you can't get rid of a Runny Polenta Hangover with water and Gorgonzola gnocchi. At work on Monday . . . and Tuesday . . . and Wednesday, the guys had to hear tell of the runny po-lenta every time someone asked how my weekend went and sometimes when they didn't. By Thursday afternoon I was still lamenting my culinary failure over drinks at happy hour, which should have been renamed "Never Happy Hour" in my honor.

As the thank you e-mails for Saturday night's dinner came in, it was everything I could do to not respond with an apology for the runny polenta. And it wasn't because I didn't think it was appropriate. Oh, I was sorry, and I really wanted them to know that. But a showbiz rule I've learned is that most people either a) don't pay attention b) have no memory or c) can't think for themselves. Therefore, when something goes wrong they either didn't notice, don't remember, or don't know it was wrong until someone tells them it was. So

I try to refrain from making excuses for mistakes and mis-steps so as to not draw attention to them in the first place.

The same thing applies to the real world, too. Just the other night I was in a parking garage, looking to pay the attendant five dollars and all I had was twenties. When I handed him one, he asked if I had something smaller and I apologized and said I didn't. That's when he looked at my hands and said, "You have a ten." Turns out not only did I have a ten, I also had a five, both of which I turned over and over again in my hands seeing only twenty dollars for some rea-son. Wishful thinking, I guess. I apologized again and said, "My God. I can't believe that. I probably shouldn't be driv-ing," which I immediately followed up with, "I mean, not that I've been drinking. I haven't. (I hadn't) It's just because I'm tired." Now, he's definitely paying attention to the nut bag in the baby blue beetle convertible and memorizing my license plate number for when he calls the cops in about two minutes. All because I had to draw attention to the fact that I thought a ten was a twenty. It's like they say in *The Godfa-ther,* just drop the gun and leave.

But it's hard. So hard.

As the thank you e-mails came in, I almost couldn't read them, because it seemed like I was receiving credit for some-thing I didn't deserve. No matter if they extolled the virtue of everything else; the wine, the cheese, the short ribs. When Remus sends me an e-mail that calls me a "fantastic cook," I think he's just trying to be nice. And I push away the mem-ory of him asking for seconds at dinner with a "He was just trying to be polite."

Yes, I know. As I type this now, it seems a little cuckoo to me, too. As does this:

About six weeks later, I have a fellow *Soup* writer and his girlfriend along with our manager and his wife over to dinner. I don't know where I found the courage to go on. And I don't know where I found the balls to do what I did: three courses, two of which were made up of homemade pasta. We had a salad, goat cheese and chicken tortelloni in a leek brodo, followed by boeuf bourguignon served over fresh fettuccine. Over dinner I found myself discussing how we were exorcising the ghost of the runny polenta.

"Were you really that upset?" my manager asked.

"Let's put it this way," my colleague interjected, "this isn't the first time I've heard this story. This isn't even the second."

At no point does it occur to me that maybe I think about things a little too much.

It's only a year and many successful dinner parties later that I am able to think about why it bothered me so deeply. Why I felt so profoundly disappointed in myself. Why that one dinner party really got to me.

I was really excited for the chance to show off my cooking: this was something I could do. As a writer, a comic, a performer, there are so few ways to quantify what it is we do; so few ways to quantify that what you do, you do well. Success isn't necessarily a good barometer, and even success is hard to quantify, there being so many levels of what you think success is. If you get a job on cable, you think, "It's not network." When you get one on network, you wish you were writing on something your friends found funny. When your friends find it funny, you wonder why no one else does and you don't have an Emmy. If you win an Emmy, you hope it makes your ratings go up so you stay on the air. And if you're on the air too long you think, "Why am I still in TV?! Why aren't I writing movies!?"

And all of the movie writers I know pretty much feel like failures, too.

I'm sure Oprah wakes up feeling like a failure because her show lasted only twenty-five years and not twenty-six.

But I have some illusion that I can quantify success at a dinner party. That there is some irrefutable formula for whether or not I am a good cook and throw a good party; that those guests who leave my house will walk away knowing beyond a doubt that I am really good at *this*.

I am a writer on a TV show with a house, a boyfriend, three cats, and two Le Creuset pots. Why do I feel I have to prove to everyone who eats at my house that I am good at something?

I cannot speak for the rest of the world, but most creative types carry around the fear that they are a fraud. That whatever "success" you've had was a fluke and everyone is looking at your boyfriend as the really talented one. And in my head I still heard the exchange between me and Remus the first time I called him for legal advice.

"I'm happy to help. You know, I want your boyfriend's business."

"You know, I'm going to be really successful one day, too."

And so I was sort of addicted to the image that I could do it all: exist in such a traditional man's world and also such a traditional woman's. Yes, I could be funny. Men could be funny. But I wanted to set myself apart. Could a man do this? Could he write the joke that made *Entertainment Weekly* this week *and* cook you a three-course pasta dinner? I wanted to stand out. I thought that food was the way.

The reality is that all I can do is honor *my* experience of the dinner party. I can think someone loved a dish and they may be lying. Conversely, I could mistake someone's silence as being unimpressed, when in fact they may have really enjoyed it. They may be too drunk to say so or mad at their husband. I can't quantify a dinner party anymore than I can quantify a script I wrote or a performance I gave. At the end of the day, all I have is whether or not I was happy with it.

In the meantime, I'm going to try my hand at homemade bread. How hard can it be?

Tip

Throwing a dinner party is like trying to juggle kittens holding flaming chainsaws and it is a miracle if you only lose an arm. The best way to avoid dropping stuff is to serve things that can be cooked or prepared ahead of time so all you have to do is plate it at the last minute. Salads and braised meats are great for this. This way you can spend most of your time drinking with your guests and boring them with vacation pictures.

Recipe
Braised Short Ribs over Polenta: All of the Flavor Without the Self-Hate

Ingredients

6 pounds short ribs

2 medium onions

2 tablespoons flour

1 bottle red wine

$\frac{1}{3}$ cup white or red vinegar

3 sprigs thyme

8 cloves garlic

1 cup dried porcini mushrooms (optional)

3 to 4 cups beef broth

Salt

Pepper

Olive oil

1 package polenta

Any type of braised meat—be it ribs or chicken or a pork loin—is perfect for a dinner party. You can prepare it before anyone gets there and then leave it to slow cook in the oven while you get dressed and entertain the guests. It's pretty much crisis proof so long as you keep it moist. As long as you do that, the meat will just get more and more tender if you find yourself having a second or third cocktail before you get around to actually serving dinner.

You're going to need a deep pan that can go from the stove top to the oven and that preferably has a lid, like a turkey roaster. I recommend Le Creuset because it's pretty. They understand a woman's desire to accessorize everything, even if it's something you will never match your shoes or bag to. Yes, it's expensive, but so are plenty of things including an engagement ring and most people have one of those. Personally, nothing says "I'll love you forever," to me like enamel coated cast-iron cookware.

Heat enough oil to cover the bottom in your pretty roasting pan and when it starts to get that shimmery effect, put your ribs (approximately 6 pounds) in the pan and brown on all sides. Don't crowd the pan. Science things happen if you don't crowd the pan that allows them to brown quickly and evenly. Or something. I don't know. Just know: crowding pan bad. Work in batches if you have to.

Also, you may want to season the ribs with salt and pepper first, but I promise you that if you forget it's not the end of the world.

As they are finished, take them out of the pan and put them on a plate. Next it's time for some onion. Brown 2 medium diced onions for about 10 minutes until all translucent and soft. You can also do carrot and celery, too, but I don't because I'm allergic.

Next, mix in 2 tablespoons of flour. Then add 3 cups of red wine, stirring to scrape up any brown bits on the bottom. Add ⅓ cup red wine vinegar, 3 or so sprigs of thyme, 8 cloves of garlic, 1 cup of dried porcini mushrooms, and 3 to 4 cups of beef broth. Bring to a boil, season with some salt and pepper, and then add the ribs back in, making sure to pour all of the juice from the plate into your pot, as well.

You're almost ready for a shower.

Cover the ribs and put them in the oven at 325°F. I roast them for 4 hours, uncovering them after the first 2, but covering them back up again if I think they're getting too browned on the top. But a little is good. I also like to check in with them every hour, make sure there's still enough liquid and give them a good stir to rotate the ones on top.

Lastly, here's a note about the braising liquid: you don't want too much. Try starting with 3 cups of wine to 3 to 4 cups of broth. You want to almost cover them entirely, but you don't want so much liquid in there that it never reduces.

Now, speaking of reducing, after the 4 hours is done, you're going to want to take the ribs out and keep them warm on a separate plate. Then you can stick the roaster back on the stove top and spoon the fat off the top—and there will be plenty. I recommend a whole cocktail just for this ordeal. *This is really the only actual cooking you will do while guests are there.* Get a pretty apron, because you don't want grease on your clothes. After you're done scraping fat, you want to simmer the sauce so as to reduce it and make it thicker, even adding some more flour if you like. But I guarantee the juice in that pan is so delicious as is, that no one will fault you if you serve it too thin.

If you want, you can even do this the day before and reheat or do what I sometimes do which is take all of the meat off the bone when it cools and scrape the fat off the top of the sauce as well. Stick it all in a pot, reduce to a ragu, and serve over anything: polenta, rice, pasta, potatoes, put it in a grilled-cheese sandwich—it's tasty.

Serve the short ribs over polenta in a shallow bowl with some au jus as a sauce. Cook the polenta according to the directions on the package.

Yield: Serves 6 people, 5 sets of DNA (and on rare occasions, 4)

Chapter 11
How to Pair Wine with Food and Which Medical Weed to Never Mix with Entertaining

While I may have finally started severing the ties between one dinner party and my entire self-esteem, The Boyfriend was just getting warmed up. It was summertime once again, so we were occupying his domain, the backyard grill. All dinner parties centered on what we could do outside, which had radically changed for the better when we learned how to do pizzas on the grill.

In a diabolical move that I can only hope to emulate one day, Mario Batali wrote a book called *Italian Grill* that featured all sorts of amazing things that could only be cooked on a marble slab, which he also conveniently sold. I'm not sure how authentically Italian the "piastra" is as I am half Italian and never once saw anyone in my family cook on one. But then again, my Italian grandmother preferred the sanctuary of a 90 degree kitchen on an 80 degree day, as if the outdoors were someplace where you caught diseases, like a strange toilet seat or a movie theater (where everyone knows you can catch lice, according to her). She needed a stone for the grill like she needed a microwave.

One of these delicious things that you could cook on the piastra was pizza. And so The Boyfriend and I made the trek out to Sur La Table to buy one. The Boyfriend was smitten. He loved grilling on the stone surface, finding it preferable to the grill or a pan to do all sorts of foods like fish and mushrooms. We were soon inventing all sorts of new and wonderful flavor combinations for pizzas: smoked Gouda with caramelized onions and sausage; garlic shrimp and goat cheese; prosciutto and truffle oil. The only problem: our dough sucked.

We had tried unsuccessfully to make it once. The Boyfriend bought quick yeast, and I have since learned that is never the way. The dough was too puffy, almost like bread, and there was so much of it! I remember trying to choke it all down without hurting his feelings. Next we found some refrigerated dough at Trader Joe's, which was nearly impossible to roll out thin enough due to its rubbery texture that just kept snapping back repeatedly. Finally I stumbled into an Italian deli that sold frozen pizza dough that actually handled like dough and tasted like pizza and every time I went in, I would buy a dozen of the balls, just so we would always have them on hand.

With our dough problem solved, our pizzas were unstoppable and we used every opportunity to make them for

guests, having grown tired of the usual grill fare: hamburgers and hot dogs or even chicken and fish. People would
break previous plans if we invited them over for pizzas and
The Boyfriend was often asked to go over to others' houses
just to cook them. Plus, everything could be customized so
that no matter what your food issue, we could accommodate you. Pizzas were perfect. There was just one thing. They
were an unholy pain in the ass.

At first they weren't so bad, probably because we were
too busy marveling at our new dish to pay attention to how
much work was involved. But in actuality, prep had to start
early in the day. The Boyfriend insisted on cooking his own
pizza sauce from scratch, and as I can't eat tomatoes, I was
in no position to tell him not to. If he said it was better, I
had to believe him. Likewise, I couldn't really assist him, as
I wouldn't be able to taste it anyway. Next there were the
toppings. Shrimp had to be cut up and marinated as did the
portobello mushrooms. This meant garlic was minced, vinaigrettes were made, and someone had to inevitably run out
for more olive oil. Tomatoes, basil, and buffalo mozzarella
had to be chopped. Goat cheese had to be taken out of its
package and sliced into smaller chunks, because if there's
one thing The Boyfriend has never mastered, it's opening
that tube of goat cheese (even the new packages that have
the convenient corner turned up). He struggles with it for a
few seconds before using something completely inappropri-
ate, not to mention dangerous, like a gigantic chef's knife to
slice it open. So I would "decant" the goat cheese early in the
day and put it in its own prep bowl, just like we did with all
of the other ingredients. Finally, if I wanted caramelized
onions, I had to cook them for nearly two hours to get the

consistency I preferred, not that I ever enjoyed them. On one occasion I forgot that I had made them and never used them. Another time, a friend knocked the glass prep bowl onto the concrete patio, before I ever got to eat them, and I had to toss the whole mess of onions and glass into the trash.... Everything except the one piece of glass that ended up lodged in The Boyfriend's foot a week later.

On top of all the prep, potential knife accidents, and gangrenous foot wounds, was the reality that pizzas could only be cooked one at a time. It quickly became very labor intensive for The Boyfriend, who was forced to spend the night chained to the grill like a wallet on a hipster. But with a small enough group it could actually become fun and social. He would stand next to the table and we would all talk and as each pizza came up he would pass it around and explain what it was. A hush would fall over everyone as they greedily ate, only taking a break to remark on how great the ingredients tasted. In between pizzas we drank wine and chatted, The Boyfriend participating while shouting out for requests. However, at other times the grill was too far away from the guests, or there were too many conversations going on at once, or the grill got too hot, or there were too many pizzas to be made and eventually The Boyfriend would find himself feeling like a short order cook and in a foul mood. But still, we kept doing it. I guess the memory of how good they tasted overshadowed the memory of how frustrated he got. Like what people always tell me about childbirth, which I have a sneaking suspicion is just propaganda to get me to join them.

But we were still somewhat in the honeymoon period of our grill pizzas when I got the bright idea to invite the *Mind of Mencia* people over. The Boyfriend had worked on the show for four years, eventually becoming the head writer and executive producer. He had started writing on the show shortly after I went to work on *The Soup*. It was those two jobs that allowed us to get our house and his time spent on the show represented a major change in our lives. When it was over he not only walked away with the best title he had to date, but with a group of really close and tight-knit friends, made up of the fellow EPs on the show. In addition to the title, they all shared a love of not just eating good food and wine, but preparing it as well.

One couple, Liz and Jack, had invited us over to their place in Burbank, but it might as well have been the south of France. We were greeted with a meat and cheese plate that featured truffle mousse, cannellini bean dip, and homemade bread. They made their own bread! They also grew many of their own fruits and vegetables and the salad was straight from their garden. For the main course we had goat cheese soufflés with a lentil and duck confit side dish and dessert was homemade crème brûlée, which was fantastic despite the fact that they had never made it before. But I'm not finished. What we were drinking most of the night was a red wine, a blend of Grenache, Syrah, and Tempranillo—THAT THEY HAD GROWN THEMSELVES! They made their own wine! One dinner with any of these couples was enough to make you step up your own game. And when you invited them for dinner, it was almost as much pressure as it was fun. Or vice versa.

However, being related to people who cook hamburger in the oven for two hours and consider salt an herb, I recognize what a joy it is to share good food and wine with people who really enjoy it, too. And it's worth it to go the extra step with people like that, because you know they'll appreciate that you did. Bottles we never opened came out with this crew and truffle honey was always put out with the cheese. And that night, we decided to do a blind wine tasting. We were going to take one of Jack's bottles from the Burbank wine region and put it up against wines with similar blends from Spain and France and California. Each one would be in a brown bag so each guest could taste them, make notes, and pick their favorite before finding out what each bottle truly was. Most people like to just get drunk. We make getting drunk a game to see who has the best palate.

A few hours before everyone arrived I suddenly remembered that the wife of one of our guests owns two restaurants, plus she spent every summer of her childhood in Italy.

I've invited a restaurateur to dinner.

Not just any restaurateur. One who's tasted her share of Italian food.

Also, just FYI, restaurateur's husband is a veteran TV producer of nearly thirty years who kept a villa in Tuscany for about twenty of them. So when he's not eating in one of his wife's two restaurants or in some of the finer dining establishments of LA, Manhattan, or The Hamptons, he's eating in small Tuscan villages.

They hadn't confirmed that they'd be attending until the day before, so I hadn't really stopped to consider her résumé before now. I had assumed they weren't coming. It occurs to me that I need to think things through more. It also occurs to me that I have to make everything extraordinary.

Fortunately, that's somewhat easier as Liz promised to bring fresh tomatoes and basil from the garden and Jack has put his bread skills to work to provide fresh pizza dough made that afternoon. In addition to the wine they made. So I guess technically now I'm cooking for a restaurateur, her villa-dwelling husband, and a two-person agriturismo. No pressure.

The prep goes smoothly and soon enough Jack and Liz are arriving with the dough and tomatoes and our friend Jim arrives with the wine, placing it into the brown bags for the blind tasting. We arrange everything on the tiki bar and start to enjoy some wine, as the other guests filter in.

Rounding out the group is Liz's sister, Krysia, her screenwriter husband, Gene, and Nikki who is stag that evening. And that's when someone—who shall remain nameless—offered up medical-grade marijuana, if anyone cared to smoke some. I declined. Pot never took with me despite years of trying to like it. It was like my brother got all of the stoner genes in the family and I just got good teeth and motivation. Besides that, we had such great wine, who wanted to ruin their perception of it with weed?! In addition to the blind tasting, Veteran TV Producer has brought a bottle of 1981 Château Lafite Rothschild that was given to him as a gift years ago, and despite it being stored in questionable conditions for many of those years, I was dying to try it.

I was standing at the bar, enjoying the wine with Liz when the offer was made.

"You're not going to smoke, are you?" she asked.

"No, I really don't get anything out of pot."

"Yeah. I don't want to smoke it if I'm drinking wine."

"Yeah," I agree, "I want to be able to enjoy the wine."

"I know," she says before pausing a moment, then, "I think I'm going to go over there and smoke some of that pot."

As you wish. After all, she was her own person who could

make choices that had no effect on me, unlike say, The Boyfriend, who incidentally I could see at that very moment taking the joint that was being offered to him.

"Are you sure you want to do that?" I ask him, as I walk over.

"Yeah. Why not?"

Why not, indeed?

While everyone else smokes pot, I busy myself with note taking, much like I did in college. Abstaining from the pot with me is Nikki, who remarks that she was never one of the cool kids, either. We're trying the wines and pouring them for others; they're all delicious and it's like Sophie's Choice to try to savor one without rushing to taste another. We're also catching up with Krysia who has just gotten in from out of town.

"Gene's not going to smoke pot, either," she confides to me. "Gene never smokes pot." That's when we look across to the tiki bar where Gene is smoking pot.

Gene is over six feet tall, but still I've rarely seen him have more than two glasses of wine without getting sleepy. And yet that pot has suddenly turned him into Tom Hulce's character from *Animal House* after the first time he gets high with Donald Sutherland and wants to know if he can buy some pot from him.

I soon feel like the only person there who is not high.

Night falls and we start the pizzas. For reasons that I'm sure were sound at the time, The Boyfriend has moved the grill away from the guests, and subsequently, the light. He is now beginning to cook in an extremely poorly lit part of the patio. In the dark. High.

Meanwhile, everyone is busy catching up, debating whether or not the '81 Lafite is any good or not. Two said, "Yes," two said, "No," while Veteran TV Producer agreed with whomever he talked to last. There's a reason he's lasted thirty years in the business. (Incidentally, I thought it was good and as I was the only person not high, I think I was right.)

The pizzas start coming out, we're cutting them up and passing them around. Everything is going swimmingly. Except everyone feels bad for The Boyfriend. One person says, "I was hoping to get to talk to him." A few people go over to him and offer him help. Here's the thing: he's not very good at telling people what he needs them to do. He either feels bad for asking anyone to do something, or he honestly doesn't know what to tell them to do. He'd have to think of it, and his attitude is that by the time he thinks of it and tells you, he could have just done it himself. He's really bad at accepting help, but extremely good at getting angry later that he didn't have any. It's a joy to live with.

Also, did I mention he was high? And not on some skank weed your sister's boyfriend grew in his dorm room; the kind someone wrote a prescription for.

So he's slaving away over a grill, incapable of accepting or asking for help, but other than the flash of guilt, we're all having a great time. Jack's pizza dough is phenomenal. It tastes even better than the stuff at the Italian deli, and it's so supple you don't even need to roll it out, you just stretch it into shape. So we don't realize The Boyfriend is having as bad a time as he is. I can see people talking to him at the grill or trying to talk to him. At least that's my perception of the evening. But what do I know? I'm not SMOKING POT!

In addition to not being skilled at accepting help, he needs to be reminded to eat while he's cooking. Guests are always saying to him, "I don't see you eating."

"I will. I will," he always insists. But he doesn't.

Finally, it's the last pizza of the night. He's saving it for himself. It's everything he wanted: sausage, pepperoni, cheese, tomatoes, basil. He takes it off the grill and places it onto the cutting board. He then—rather than walk the cutting board over to the table or even inside the house to a suitable flat, level, hard surface—balances the cutting board on top of a cement ledge about six inches square and proceeds to run the pizza cutter over it, pressing too hard on the unsupported end, toppling the cutting board and sending his pizza to the ground.

We all feel terribly. Everyone feels awful. And yet there is nothing to do. A small consolation is that he has just enough ingredients left that he can make one last pizza for himself, that he can at least eat, but it is certainly not the masterpiece that is lying all over the patio right now.

At times like this he needs some quiet alone time.

Fortunately, it's getting unseasonably cold and we all move inside for dessert. Jim keeps him company and eventually The Boyfriend comes in to eat his dinner, close to midnight. Other than his unhappiness, the dinner is a success. Rather than leave the party, Liz is allowing her husband to fall asleep while sitting up at the table. Nikki has brought the most gorgeously decorated cupcakes along with gelato and we all feel decadent as we dig in. When everyone offers me help with the dishes, I know to accept and we knock out the dozen or so plates and wineglasses quickly.

Hosting dinner parties doesn't just make you a good

host, it eventually makes you a good guest, as well. You understand all the things you wish your guests would do to make the night go smoother. Sometimes it's just a matter of showing up on time. Someone's got to be that first person in the door, and if I know I'm going to have to depart early, I try to make that person me. Also, pitching in with the dishes is a huge help. Yes, you can ask if the host would like some help, and more often than not they will demur and say, "No, thank you." That's our job as a host. But as the guest, every once in a while you need to just get in there with someone else and say, "I'll wash and you dry," and not take no for an answer. Believe me the host will make it known if that is her antique china that she wants no one but herself to handle—and then you can back away from the dishes and enjoy another glass of wine guilt free.

These were all good hosts, hence they were great guests as well and it was after one when the last ones left.

The next morning The Boyfriend and I wake up slowly after such a late night. I'm in a slightly foul mood as I have been waking up every hour or so throughout the night, only to discover that the log we were burning in the outdoor fireplace is still not out. Despite its three-hour maximum burn time and the copious amounts of water I have poured on it, a flame continues to rise out of the ashes like some sort of phoenix that is fucking with me. It is summertime in a desert known for its raging wildfires. What looked beautiful in the center of the patio last night, now looks like a potential lawsuit as I keep waking with the fear that we are going to burn down all of the San Fernando Valley. I can see the newspaper's headline: SOUTHERN CALIFORNIA COMEDY COUPLE STARTS INFERNO AFTER BOYFRIEND GETS TOO

HIGH WHILE MAKING PIZZAS. We're lying in bed, discussing what we might do with our day and I'm explaining to him that I'm grumpy and tired after a night of volunteer fire-fighting.

"You know I'm not in such a great mood myself," he says. "I'm not happy with how things went last night."

He then starts sending e-mails. It turns out they're letters of apology.

"Why are you apologizing?"

"Everyone had such a bad time last night," he explains.

"Everyone had a great time last night!" I insist, incredulous. I also maybe said, "You're nuts," a few times.

"No, they didn't. They were bored and sitting around waiting for the food all night."

"Oh my God, I can't believe you would even think that! They were having such a great time no one wanted to go! Jack fell asleep at the table because Liz didn't want to go." I may have also said, "You're nuts!" a few more times for good measure.

"No, they were miserable," he maintains, before out of nowhere saying, "You know that pot was great! Usually it makes me paranoid. But not last night."

Tip

A good host always serves himself, too. No one likes a cranky host who martyrs himself by serving everyone in front of him so that his blood sugar drops and then when he finally eats he is so shaky from drinking on an empty stomach that he spills his food all over the patio, screaming obscenities. Likewise, a good host knows when to ask for help and graciously accepts when it is offered. If we want our dinner with a side of uncomfortable resentment, we'll go home for the holidays.

Chapter 12
How to Cook Without Cooking

It was our anniversary.

So of course I was in tears in the middle of the restaurant.

To be fair, we had celebrated our anniversary the weekend before. We had gone to a beachfront resort and rented a cabana and read novels while young men in polo shirts brought us drinks. It was lovely. This was our bonus dinner since it was the *actual* day of our anniversary, and despite it being a weeknight, we were both free. It seemed silly to sit at home, even if in retrospect that might have been a better call.

We were eating at a local place that I had been to about eight dozen times in the mere six months it had been open. The attraction was the owner from Naples and the best truffle pizza in town. Enzo was very patient with me as I attempted speaking Italian to him, which I sometimes got better at the more I drank. Also, it was about ten minutes from our house and we were thrilled to have a restaurant we liked in the neighborhood. Since we bought at the height of the market, all the houses in good restaurant neighborhoods were out of our price range.

The conversation turned toward the upcoming Labor Day weekend. Labor Day weekend was always a tough one for us. We had the pool, so naturally we wanted to see our friends and swim and have one last great weekend outdoors. Even though it could be hot through November in LA, we had found over the years that people just stop wanting to swim after Labor Day. It's a psychological switch ingrained from twelve to twenty years of education that followed the school year calendar. Personally, I still find it baffling that after all of those years of having summers off and a few weeks at Christmas, the world expects you to just adapt and go to work during the very same times your body knows it should be on vacation. Conversely, after Labor Day happens, something inside of us knows to get to work, whether it's painting the bathroom or writing a novel. People who had spent the summer lounging in the pool every weekend with a drink in their hand, were suddenly getting down to business and unavailable by the 8th of September.

Naturally, then, we wanted one last celebration of the summer. However, what made it hard was that Labor Day always fell on or near our anniversary. We were always perplexed as to how to work in both our need to celebrate the summer with our friends and our desire to celebrate the anniversary with each other. Thus, having celebrated our anniversary the weekend before officially, Labor Day this year should have been easy. Should have.

I wanted things to be easy. Over the four years we had

been in the house, we had already pared down the guest list considerably from the eighty or so people we had invited to our first Labor Day party. Gone were the people who refused to leave at three in the morning. Gone were the people who refused to watch their kids by the pool. Gone were the people who refused to play well with others, alienating them either by getting too drunk or being ridiculously confrontational or sad and morose or freaking them out by telling horrible childbirth stories. We had finally reduced our invites to a small group of core friends, people who were good guests, brought even better wine, and who all got along—or at least could fake it for the summer. This should help matters immensely as we decided to have one last outdoor party for the year.

The Boyfriend insisted there be food. He always insists there be food. I don't know how he's Irish, since clearly he acts as if he were raised by a pack of feral Jewish and Italian mothers. I knew that since we'd be out by the pool, the food in question would be the grill, and the "weed usually makes me paranoid" pizza incident was still fresh in my mind. However, it wasn't like making something else would be any different. He was too much of a perfectionist; hamburgers were just as rife with stress for him. Here's what would happen:

Persons A, B, and C would tell The Boyfriend that they would want burgers. Person A would want cheese, Person B would want it medium rare, and Person C wanted a veggie burger, *all of which The Boyfriend was fine with.* But then they would walk away. I don't blame them; who wants to stand next to a grill when it's 90 degrees out? How about the guy cooking for you? The Boyfriend would inevitably get very aggravated, because when the burgers were done, Persons A, B, and C were nowhere to be found. A person with a healthy level of stress would then just stick the burgers on the plate, tell people they were finished, and then walk away. But The Boyfriend does not have a healthy level of stress. He would be upset that the burgers he had worked hard to cook well were getting cold and ruined. Or he would find that Person A had never eaten their burger or Person C couldn't find theirs and needed a new one. Or sometimes someone whose kid had been swimming the entire afternoon despite the fact that the rest of us were eating, would announce to him right as he was shutting down the grill that their child was hungry. To which a person with a healthy stress level would have just told everyone, "Tough shit." But that's not The Boyfriend's style.

I don't blame him. Frequently we would discuss the barbeques we went to where the host just cooked up a bunch of hot dogs and hamburgers and left them on a plate next to the grill for the rest of the afternoon for whoever wanted one. Just a stack of burgers getting cold and hard and dry, that the flies didn't even want to touch. Who the hell would want to eat that? I didn't. But I bet *that* host's girlfriend wasn't crying in the middle of a restaurant on their anniversary, either.

So we had a dilemma. . . .

The irony was that discussing menus and making cooking plans used to be fun. True, we had spent our early years cooking out of financial necessity. But we always knew what good food was and enjoyed creating it. Many of the standards in our own home had come from trying new dishes while at restaurants and thinking, "I wonder if I can make this . . . ?" And then we'd get home and try, learning from each experience, and attempting to perfect it until we'd be out at that same restaurant thinking, "I like ours better." We still enjoyed it, when we had the time to relax enough to think anything was fun. They say time = money. In my experience, when you have a lot of time, you probably don't have a lot of money, and vice versa.

What had once brought us together was threatening to tear us apart and that weekend I wanted to avoid The Boyfriend cooking at all costs. So much so, in fact, that I found myself in tears despite having a slice of the City's Most Awesome Truffle Pizza in front of me. And my tears were forcing him to say, "Just tell me what you want then."

"I want you to promise me you won't touch the grill all weekend."

"Fine," he conceded, "I won't touch the grill all weekend."

That settled, we now only had to figure out what we actually were going to serve our guests. I had solved one problem, only to create another. The idea of fried chicken was tossed around. Edie had given me a great recipe for oven-fried chicken the year before and I thought I could make a big batch the day before and serve it cold. But I think in the final analysis, we realized this was just trading one day's cooking headaches for another. Ordering pizza was suggested before getting shot down because there were no great pizza places that delivered near us.

We weren't in a great problem-solving place. The earlier drama of the night hadn't put either of us in a particularly receptive mood. That's why we knew it must be a good idea when I said, "What about grilled cheeses like at Lois's baby shower?" and The Boyfriend looked genuinely intrigued.

What makes a great entertainer is not always about

being a great cook. In fact sometimes what makes you a great entertainer is not cooking at all because being a great entertainer is recognizing your limits so that you don't become a stressed-out wreck who all of your guests are afraid of. That tends to make you a _bad_ entertainer.

There was another reason I needed this to be easy: our Fourth of July that year had pushed me over the edge. This time, The Boyfriend's stress levels had nothing to do with it, at least not directly. To begin with, I was suffering from a particularly nasty bout of acid reflux, always brought on from stress (so perhaps he had something to do with it). Because of the reflux, I wasn't drinking much, which I don't recommend if your friends are going to ACT LIKE ASSHOLES.

To begin with, Sabrina—due to what we'll just call a bad reaction to some medication—bluntly told one of our friends that the show he wrote on had lost her as a viewer and that she was giving it four episodes of the upcoming season before she was done forever. Happy Fourth of July. Just because our forefathers wanted us to have free speech, doesn't mean that they intended for us to use it to ruin other people's pool parties.

She approached me in the kitchen where I was pouring myself another glass of water, the last one still burning a hole in my throat as if it had been pure whiskey.

"Tess..." she started in her baby voice, which always means trouble, "I did something bad."

I downed my firewater wishing it _were_ whiskey.

Nowhere near fortified, I asked, "What happened?" I needed clarification. Doing "something bad" to Sabrina could mean any number of things from buying an expensive purse to doing cocaine and staying up all night reading *Harry Potter*.

Sabrina continued in her baby voice, which should really be analyzed in therapy someday, to tell me a slightly softer version of what she had said to our friend Justin, whose girlfriend had just walked into the kitchen in time to overhear the whole exchange. I looked at the girlfriend, I looked at Sabrina, then back to the girlfriend, who was awkwardly inching backward out of the kitchen like a cartoon character. I really wished I could drink.

Here's a tip: if you like to start shit, don't have a catchphrase. When Justin later recounted his version of the incident to me, he quoted Sabrina as saying, "I'm sorry. I know that's not nice. But I never said I was a nice girl." Busted. Up until then, I was trying to be fair giving both of my good friends the benefit of the doubt. I really tried hard to imagine how this was just a big, drunken misunderstanding. But I knew that quote. I had heard her say it before. If you want plausible deniability in a "he said, she said," don't have a catchphrase. You might as well be a serial killer with a signature.

While I was wishing I could drink, one friend was kind enough to drink for both of us. I had been watching Jill's alcohol intake all day with growing concern. Not like, "She has a problem concern." Just, "She's going to have to spend the night," concern. I have no problem if you want to get stinking, sad-Irish-dad-in-*Angela's Ashes* drunk at my house as long as you don't drive yourself home or vomit on my linens. That's my cats' job. But I had known from previous experiences that Jill wasn't always good about knowing her limits or pacing herself. When once the year before, The Boyfriend and I had suggested she slow down around 5 a.m., she said without guile, "OK, I'll switch to beer." And why is it that the worst drunks I know have to sleep in their own beds at night? If you like to drink without pacing yourself, you should always carry a spare toothbrush and get used to other people's futons.

As I saw that it was getting later and she wasn't slowing down, I suggested to her that she should probably stop if she was going to drive. When that didn't happen, I took to throwing out her drinks whenever she went to the bathroom or wasn't paying attention, which wasn't that hard, given her level of intoxication. Eventually she caught on to what was happening and just got another one. Finally, when she was ready to leave, I asked The Boyfriend to say something, as my protestations just fell on drunk, deaf ears. He followed her out to her car where he eventually got her to come in and sit down. She did as he asked, giving me the cold shoulder the whole time. It went nicely with my burning-hot esophagus.

The day after the party, our friend Frank died.

By the time I had woken up and learned the news, Jill had already sent me a text, an e-mail, and a voice-mail, not apologizing for the night before, but thanking me and telling me what a wonderful time she had. I knew it was her way of feeling out the situation to see if I was pissed, without having to cop to doing something that might have pissed me off. By her second phone call, I knew I had to respond so I texted her to tell her I had received her messages, but that

Frank had died and I couldn't talk. She wrote back to say that she was sorry for our loss and that if I wanted to go out and drown my sorrows and needed a designated driver, to give her a call.

"Why?" I wanted to write back. "Do you know someone?"

After that I was done. By Labor Day my reflux was under control and I wanted to keep it that way. No more bullshit. Sabrina was still in: she had been appropriately contrite, gotten her meds under control, and in the final analysis the whole thing hadn't been that big of a deal. Also she's my trainer and this ass ain't going to torture itself. And maybe I gained a little perspective, too. Sabrina wasn't the first person to piss someone off with their opinions in my backyard, and she certainly wouldn't be the last; it wasn't my responsibility. And perhaps more importantly, opinionated people weren't going to kill someone on the way home from my house. Jill, however, was off the list for Labor Day.

We now had all of the ingredients for a peaceful and relaxing Labor Day, which is exactly what we had.

The Boyfriend diligently set up the grilled-cheese station. Due to the intense heat outside, we decided that highly perishable food items such as cheese and aiolis would be best kept inside. The setup was similar to Lois's shower. There were stacks of different types of breads and cheeses along with fantastic condiments such as sun-dried tomatoes, honey, and mustard. The Boyfriend had left a note at the buffet urging our guests to not cross-contaminate the various spreads and garnishes because of my allergies. This sweet display of thoughtfulness was all I needed to put the stress of the day, the week, and the summer behind me. I put my bikini on and poured myself a drink, ready to finally relax.

It was a manageable group of just twelve of us. As people arrived they were given instructions: when they were hungry they were to help themselves and make the sandwich of their choosing inside, and then come out to the tiki bar, where we had placed two panini makers, to cook it. They could eat whatever, whenever, as long as The Boyfriend and I didn't have to cook. The pressure off, we were able to just kick back and relax, having a few cocktails and enjoying our guests and our pool. And our friends were so understanding about our need to not cook, that everyone went out of their way to bring delicious things to snack on, serve on the side, or have for dessert.

Eventually people got hungry for something more than rice chips and hummus, and started to migrate inside to prepare their grilled cheeses. As people sat on the edge of the pool eating their freshly grilled sandwiches, everyone couldn't wait to hear what combinations we had all created. Excitedly, people would say, "I'm going to try that next," or offer to trade halves with another person. The Boyfriend and I had created a unique, culinary experience that everyone was talking about, all without turning on a burner or dropping food all over the patio.

A good host thanks their guests. The week after the party I sent everyone an e-mail.

I just wanted to thank you guys for being such a great group of guests. We had such a fantastic and relaxing time on Saturday and it was so due to you guys. Not only did everyone bring plenty of delicious things, but you were all always willing to pitch in whether it was helping yourselves, each other, or The Boyfriend, and me. I know it seems silly, but it really is the little things.

If you're going to be a serial entertainer, then it's important to have a solid group of serial guests and to show them some gratitude for being gracious and fun and above all, great friends. It really is the little things.

Tip

Know your limits. Learn from your past dinner parties. Don't do the things that bring you no joy or make you downright hostile. You can still have a wonderfully fun gathering by finding creative— yet reasonable—solutions to things that haven't worked in the past.

Recipe
Setting Up a
Grilled-Cheese Station:
How to Make Your Guests
Cook Their Own Food

Ingredients
Bread
Cheese
Condiments

This is so easy, you're going to feel guilty. You're going to feel guilty as hell as you merely decant bread from its bag or simply stick a spoon into an open jar of mustard. And if you feel guilty then, you will feel Single-Mom-Leaving-for-Business-Trip guilty when your friends rave about it and ask for seconds and tell you it's the best thing they've ever eaten.

But you know what else you will feel? Relaxed. And probably pleasantly buzzed.

All you need is one or more panini makers and lots of counter or table space for your sandwich station. Then all you have to do is go to the store and use your imagination. Start with your bread and your cheese. Choose some basics: a hearty white or sourdough bread for purists; a neutral cheese like a mild cheddar or provolone. You want something for less adventurous eaters, however that doesn't mean this is the time for cheese that comes individually wrapped. (It is never the time for individually wrapped slices of cheese!) After that's out of the way, get some blue cheese, some goat, some sharp cheddar, some Gouda. You can buy this whole and slice or grate yourself or you may be able to find gourmet cheeses such as these already sliced, at places like Trader Joe's. Get some wheat breads, something a little eccentric like olive bread or cinnamon. Remember to buy the appropriate amount for your guests. There may be six loaves at the store you're dying to try, but if you're only serving twelve people that may be overkill. What are you going to do with the leftovers, besides create the biggest flock of foodie pigeons on your block?

Next, if you want, you can always add different meats like prosciutto or salami or braised short ribs. But braised short ribs take work (see chapter 10) so you may want to skip this. Or do as we do, and next time you braise some short ribs, throw a little meat and gravy into the freezer for days like this.

After that, pick some spreads: mustards, honeys, aiolis,

tapenades. The gourmet food section at the grocery story is your oyster! Raid the gift baskets you got last Christmas for those condiments you never thought you'd use. Depending on how much work you personally want to do, you could slice up some tomatoes, fry some bacon, or caramelize some onions. Pick up a few things like walnuts or currants or raisins. Put a bowl of potato chips out so that people can crush up potato chips on their sandwich like they're five again. Remember, if it sounds good to you, it will probably sound good to others as well. And if it doesn't, it still sounds good to you, so who cares?

Arrange everything in some semblance of easy to get to order and try to have a separate spoon or fork for everything for people who are allergic to half of those things, such as myself. Then just plug in the panini makers and you're all ready to go! I know, it's so simple but so delicious, people won't even mind that you're making them cook their own food.

Chapter 13
How to Cook a Gluten-Free Vegetarian Dinner with No Lactose or Fruits or Vegetables or Nuts

It had been a challenging year.

It was December and me and the five guys who made up our writing staff were nearing the end of our sixth season on *The Soup*. It was six years of seeing the same faces five days a week, forty-nine weeks a year. Six years of petty squabbles over where to eat lunch. Six years of not wanting to laugh too hard at someone else's joke before they laughed at yours. Six years of watching the same, mind-numbing, soul-crushing reality TV shows. I wanted to celebrate.

A word about our writing staff: very few shows are in production continuously for forty-nine weeks a year. Sure, we got a one week reprieve in the summer (last year we got two!) but other than that, we were together day in and day out, 245 days a year times six. I don't know if you've ever hung out with any writers, but our charm wears off halfway through the second drink. The majority of us had been there the full six years. The "new guy" had been there five. Most marriages don't last this long. And we were all staring down Year Seven.

Having said all that, I am madly and deeply in love with these guys.

Six years is a serious chunk of time in anyone's life and ours were no different. In six years the six of us had experienced many milestones together: two marriages, the birth of two kids, the death of one parent, four houses purchased, and one accidental Xanax overdose. We confided in each other when we were having problems, leaned on each other when we were deflated, and laughed together every single day. We busted balls and took care of each other all at the same time. Also, we ate together.

We didn't eat together every day. Sure, there'd be the occasional run to get food together with another writer, sometimes we'd even sit down together, but for the most part we were a very independent group who kept to their own schedules and chose to eat at their desk. But one day a week we'd have a two-hour window in the middle of a twelve- or thirteen-hour day. We had delivered that week's script and there was nothing pressing to do for a few hours until we found out the show was too long, and stuff needed to be cut, or that clip wasn't working and needed to be replaced. And so, we'd eat.

Whereas the average lunch for Ye Olde Comedy Writers

of Yore was a slice of pizza or an eight ball of cocaine, these were serious sit-down lunches. We had all come to have a real appreciation for food and wine, and so restaurants were disregarded if we didn't like their wine list. We were constantly on the lookout for someplace new, having not liked "the way that last place cooked my steak," or "their poulet rôti has slipped." And of course we couldn't agree on any one place. At any given time two of us weren't eating carbs, one writer was lactose intolerant, and I had my own food allergy issues. But we persevered because this lunch was really important to us as individuals and a group. It was where we went to decompress from getting the show together, where we bitched about everything that had irritated us during that week and where we caught up and were friends. Over time I realized that there were many other things I could have been doing with those two hours every week. But few would have been as important.

That year, beyond the usual feeling that we were all on a submarine together, Joel had started *Community*, leaving the rest of us to feel like Dad got remarried and the new kids were younger and cuter. I don't mean to say that he was different; despite the fact that he was trying to juggle two full-time jobs and a family, he was actually a peach. And I don't want it to sound like we weren't happy for him. We had worked alongside of him for six years building this franchise and were very happy that he was getting a big break. But for some of us there was the nagging question, "Where was our big break?" We had spent six years at the same job and while that's a luxury that many writers don't get, we couldn't help wonder what the next thing was for us. When were *our* careers going to move ahead?

Also that year the Writers Guild had come a-calling, wanting to organize our show and a bunch of others. For the record I will say that I'm pro union and I think they're a great thing for this country. "Union organization" however, is a phrase made up of two seemingly related words that have nothing to do with the job at hand. There was no "unity" to the way anybody involved thought, just conflict and stress. Often I would ride home from work with Fid, our "shop steward," having the same argument I had had with him on the way there—only between morning and night we had totally switched positions on whatever piece of strategy or demand we were arguing about. Suffice it to say, I'm pretty sure even Norma Rae wouldn't have said that organizing that cotton mill was a lot of fucking fun and it wasn't for us, either.

So as we were limping to the end of the year, heads full of doubt about our futures and questions about things called the "National Labor Board," I wanted to do something to lift our collective morale and I went with what I knew. I wanted us to eat together. It was one of the things we did best. The Boyfriend and I invited the writers and their various lady friends over for a holiday dinner, a night of eating good food, and opening great bottles of wine.

Everybody was in and, for men, seemingly excited. That was good enough for me! That left the menu to plan. I think I had settled on braised lamb shank because I had repeatedly bragged to Lee that I made a really good one and he had to try mine sometime. I had just perfected it the Christmas Eve before, getting the braising juices just the right consistency so as to make a great gravy for both the meat and the mushroom risotto I served it with. It was the perfect winter meal:

gamey and hearty and would pair great with the big red wines I knew we'd all be drinking.

I decided to do this despite the fact that I knew Lee's wife didn't eat red meat. Not a problem: I would make her some coq au vin separately.

Also, Darren and Fid's wife, were both lactose intolerant. Again, not a problem: we would reserve some of the risotto before we put the cheese in and place it in a separate pot for them.

Then, a week or two before the dinner, we were at lunch and K.P. casually mentions that his wife has a gluten allergy. Not like, "Hey, heads up since you're cooking for us in a week," mentions it. It was more like, "You know since she realized she had the gluten thing she's been feeling so much better...."

This was news to me, who had shared many meals with his wife over the ten years I had known her. "Wait, what gluten thing?"

"Oh, she's got a gluten allergy. Been off of it for months."

"Good to know," I said out loud, while thinking "Fuck!" on the inside. I now had to find a way to thicken the lamb reduction, the very thing that I had perfected the year before, without using flour.

And that's when Darren's girlfriend went all vegetarian on me.

Six months earlier she'd been a guest in my house while I served boeuf bourguignon. Now he was telling me that she didn't eat any meat, not even the coq au vin I was making for Lee's wife.

"She'll be fine with just sides," he said.

Sides!? I'm not going to invite someone to my house and

serve them sides! This isn't a Boston Market! I won't even let people drink cheap booze in my presence. I'm not going to throw an elegant dinner party for twelve people and let one of them eat "just sides."

Reexamining the facts, I realized I might have to let her eat just sides.

Even if on top of the separate risottos, the coq au vin, and the somehow gluten-free-thickened braised lamb shank, I was able to cook something else, I didn't know what that would be. What is the main course for a vegetarian? By definition, isn't everything they eat just a side, really?

You may be asking yourself, "Why am I doing this?" Why am I making two and three separate things, researching gluten-free thickening agents, sick over a vegetarian having to eat sides? Because people do it for me. No one is a bigger pain in the ass to cook for than me. Let's refresh: no fruit, no nuts, and no to a varied and erratic list of vegetables. And let's not even get into the fact that I have an irrational fear of mayonnaise. (To be clear not aioli, the mixing together of garlic, olive oil, and egg; mayonnaise, the gelatinous, jarred mixture of God only knows what, something that resembles a misplaced specimen jar of rhino semen.) People have been inviting me over for years, despite my protests that they'd be sorry later. They have always tried to accommodate my ridiculousness and so I try to accommodate others. Because I know better than anyone, just because you can't eat certain things—nay just because you can't enjoy entire food groups—is no reason that you can't enjoy food. That doesn't mean that you cannot know the sublime, bang your fist down on a table and say, "That's stupid it's so good" pleasure of a good meal. And it is certainly no reason you shouldn't get to enjoy that pleasure with friends.

The week before the dinner, I have settled on arrowroot as my gluten-free thickening agent, with cornstarch as my backup, although I have never used either and I'm increasingly nervous as I can't find anywhere how much you should use per cup or quart of liquid. I buy three packets of arrowroot, a pricey proposition at something like six dollars an ounce, and hope that's enough. It's not the most expensive spice in the aisle. That would be saffron, a spice so expensive that inside the bottle they package it inside an even smaller plastic envelope, as if it's some uncut China White heroin and the good people at the Whole Foods spice factory are sitting around weighing and packaging it naked to be sure that no one walks home with some.

So far I'm making the braised lamb shank, coq au vin, mushroom risotto, braised leeks, and now that I know about the gluten thing, a flourless chocolate cake for dessert. And then one day in the car, Fid started talking about pie.

"You know we've been making pies recently . . . ," he started. Fid was from the Midwest and had this way of pausing when he was talking that made it seem as if he was deeply pondering what you were discussing, when really it was just a lingering side effect of some windowpane acid he took at a Black Sabbath concert in 1978. But as discussing pies was much preferable to discussing union activity, I let him take his time, waiting to see how this was going to pan out.

"You know they're not that hard. . . ."

"No, it's not that hard at all. In fact it's remarkably easy once you know what you're doing. In fact I don't know why people even bother with store-bought. I make pies all the time. I was thinking of making a pie next week for dinner," I prattled on, trying to fill the large, LSD-size crater in the conversation.

"Yeah," he continues, "we did an apple pie last weekend............"

"..Few weeks ago we made a cherry pie. . . ."

"You know......we're planning on making one this weekend.........we could bring it to your house."

Finally, a cogent thought!

I thanked him and told him that was very thoughtful but assured him that he didn't need to bring anything. I was inviting everyone else to dinner and didn't want them to feel obligated.

"It's no trouble. . . . We were going to do it anyway. . . . Doesn't take any time. . . ."

We went back and forth a few more times, me saying I didn't want to trouble him, him saying it was no trouble after a few hallucinogenic pauses. But then I realized that just like one of the pleasures of a big dinner for me was creating it, sharing in the prep may increase the enjoyment for others as well. Didn't I love going to someone's house for dinner and being asked to bring something? Didn't I enjoy making something that I loved? Wasn't I flattered when we were all gathered around the table eating so much good food and someone spoke up about how much they liked something of mine? Doesn't contributing to the dinner further enforce the communal experience you're looking to create around the table? How could I rob my guests of that experience?

I doubt Fid gave it as much thought as I did. But he did say he'd bring a pie that Sunday.

A similar exchange happened when Darren offered to bring a salad earlier in the week. Having just learned to make various vinaigrettes the year before, they were now sort of The Boyfriend's thing and he was going to make a salad of winter greens. But after my "Fid-piphany," I realized it was my job as hostess to encourage people to take part in the preparation and learn to love cooking good food. So I told him he could bring a salad, that would be much appreciated, thank you.

I spent the entire weekend prepping for the dinner. On Friday I shopped. Saturday, I made the flourless chocolate cake and braised the leeks. Sunday morning I was up early. I had a detailed schedule for when things had to be prepped to go into the oven. I crushed herbs to flavor pitchers of water. I laid out the meat and cheese plate, carefully labeling each of the cheeses so the lactose intolerant would know which ones were goat's milk and acceptable, and which ones weren't. I set the table, taking half an hour to arrange the place cards around it trying to figure out who would be a good fit around the writer's girlfriend none of us had ever met. But I wasn't rushed or resentful or overwrought. As I said in the introduction, there is something about all of this that makes me want to do it. There's something I enjoy . . . in fact, more than one. I like the orderliness of setting a table. Counting first twelve placemats, then twelve plates, then twelve water glasses. I like getting creative by taking something I have lying around the house like pinecones, and making them place card holders. I like the way the water tastes when it's flavored with basil and mint. And I like standing back at the end when it's all finished and taking in the pretty scene I've created. It's pleasing to me and I feel a sense of accomplishment. And in a way, it's meditative. I'm never going to be the type of person who can sit on a mat and chant and quiet their mind. I can't make my mind go blank; that only happens when I really need to be witty and charming. If you want me to quiet my mind without benefit of a drink in my hand, best to let me set the table. And who am I kidding? I'm still probably doing it with a drink in my hand.

But before too long the quiet has stopped and the guests are arriving. After much fanfare Fid arrives with a pie in hand—a store-bought pie in hand. I tried to not look confused . . . or disappointed.

"I thought you wanted to make one?" Actually you insisted to me for an entire car ride that you wanted to make one.

"Yeah, well . . . we didn't have time. . . ."

I didn't have an hour to get specifics on what that meant. Fortunately, just then, Darren walked in and handed me a grocery bag of greens and a bottle of salad dressing.

The men fared better with the booze. In addition to the bottles of red Darren and Nic had brought, Nic had brought a port and K.P. a bottle of scotch and two bottles of Barolo. Clearly this was going to be a good night, no matter how the food tasted, which was good because the arrowroot wasn't thickening the lamb at all, hippie-gluten substitutes be damned.

The plan was cocktails at 6:30, dinner at 7:30. Only at 7:30, a writer who I will not name lest I shame him in print, had still not shown up. He had texted to say they were having sitter issues but were on their way. Unfortunately, they were also the couple coming the farthest. That's when K.P.'s wife explained, that due to their sitter issues, she had to be home by 9:30. It made perfect sense. Three hours seems like plenty of time for dinner, if everyone else shows up on time. I poured another drink and tried to console myself with the knowledge that this would just give the lamb more time to not thicken.

Back in the kitchen, The Boyfriend is starting the risotto. Earlier in the day, while I was just casually doing some reading on better and more difficult ways to cook things, I shared with The Boyfriend a technique for cooking risotto, where you cook the dry rice in the pan before you add the liquid.

"That sounds like a lot of work," he said curtly.

"I'm not saying we should try it tonight," I began.

"Good because that sounds like a lot of work."

"I know it sounds like a lot of work," I responded. "That's why I'm not saying we should do it tonight!"

"I'm just saying it sounds like a lot of work."

"I know!" I was exasperated, anxious to end the conversation.

"I mean I can do it if you want . . ."

"I don't want!"

"Good, because it sounds like a lot of work."

That settled the matter. Clearly. Because when I walked into the kitchen he was cooking the risotto in that way, the one that sounded like a lot of work.

Finally around 8:30, Lee—shit, there I go naming him and shaming him in print—arrives and I race to get dinner on the table. I tell Darren that now is the time to prepare his salad.

"Oh, I don't know how to do that," he says.

I pull The Boyfriend away from the risotto to complete the salad and then I go about wondering what to do with the lamb. Here's what I should have done: I should have put a lamb shank and some broth aside and kept it warm and then thickened the rest of it with a buerre manié, a mixture of flour and butter. Here's what I did: nothing. My experiment with arrowroot a failure, I lacked the clarity to think things through to the clear solution. The Barolo was very good.

The salad is served and as I don't eat the salad, I take that time while everyone is eating to start plating the food. Only by now it's 9:30. As I am plating the gluten-free lamb shank, K.P.'s wife comes in to apologize profusely and say that she has to leave and relieve her sitter.

I promise to send her husband home with some gluten-free lamb shank. Also, the flourless chocolate cake.

After walking her to the door and clearing the salad plates on the table, I walk back into the kitchen to see The Boyfriend putting the finishing touches on the risotto, ladling lamb stock into the pot.

He's ladling lamb stock into the risotto. The risotto, in case you don't know, is technically a side dish. In fact one of two side dishes that Darren's vegetarian girlfriend will be eating as her supper this evening.

If you're keeping track, so far I'm serving a runny braised lamb shank, vegetarian risotto with lamb broth, and a store-bought pie. But the coq au vin looks delicious!

We get all of the food plated and to the table and are just about to sit down. The pitchers of water I have taken great pains to flavor with basil and mint are slowly making their way around the table. As the last one reaches me, I tip it over my glass only to watch nothing come out. It is completely empty, all of the basil-mint water sitting in everyone else's glass. You've got to be kidding me.

Luckily, things were about to get worse.

Everyone else at the table is looking to the head of the table, waiting for their hosts to sit down so they can start eating. And in the silence, that's when it happened.

"I don't hear any music."

That was the voice of Lee. He was teasing me because he knows that I have a ridiculous obsession with Christmas music. But he stepped on a land mine. What he didn't know was that the music situation in the house turned The Boyfriend into Darren McGavin from *A Christmas Story* every time the heater acts up, and he was already pretty tightly wound to begin with. Over the years we had tried to find a solution to wirelessly stream music from our computers to several AirPorts and one Apple TV. What we ended up with was a system that randomly cut out and often stopped altogether for no apparent reason despite years of marathon phone calls to AppleCare. It would have been less tense if Lee had discussed unspeakable acts he personally performed on each and every one of The Boyfriend's ex-girlfriends while calling him an unfunny hack.

Aggravated, The Boyfriend gets up from the table in a huff and walks into the office, where our technology is housed. Everyone is still staring at me, wondering when they can eat, and also probably what just happened as we are at the far end of the table. I encourage everyone to start eating and go into the office to retrieve my cohost and sweet-talk him back to the table.

"What are you doing!?"

"The music isn't playing so I have to reboot the entire system."

"No one cares about that. No one can even hear the music. There's twelve people in there, six of them writers! We only want to hear the sounds of our own voices. We can't even hear each other!"

"No, it's fine. It's fine. It's just going to take me awhile."

"Come on," I plead. "No one wants to eat until you're seated."

He's still not budging, refusing to leave the office. I try one last ditch effort.

"Really?" I say in not really a stage whisper. "Do you want us to be these people now!?"

Back at the table Lee's wife turns to him. "Go in there and say something."

Nic also turns to Lee, "Dude, no really. Don't get involved."

She insists, "Lee, go in there!"

Nic insists, "Really, dude, not a good idea."

Not being married to Nic, Lee walks into the office for one brief moment.

"I was just kidding. Please come eat."

But The Boyfriend asks us to leave him alone. Lee gives up and a moment later, so do I.

I don't remember if the music played after that or not.

When he finally comes back to the table, he's short and it's awkward and uncomfortable. Eventually—either when someone started talking shit about another writer who's success is grossly disproportional to his talent, or maybe when K.P. gave us our Christmas presents—things loosen up and we all move on. The night is, for the most part, a success.

The Boyfriend is several glasses of wine and probably a

scotch removed from the music incident when the last of our guests leave and he joins me in the kitchen for cleanup. I am livid. Over the years I had been hurt and angry over a myriad of his perceived transgressions, all of which had various degrees of my own complicity. But I don't think I had ever felt I had quite the moral high ground as that night. I had worked so hard on this dinner. He had seen me work for *days* on this dinner. This wasn't about our morale as a staff, this was about my morale. I was the one unsure of her future, the one looking for a way out of the rut. He took all of my hard work and ruined it, choosing instead to put his own frustration with a STUPID PIECE OF TECHNOLOGY WHOSE SOLE PURPOSE IN LIFE IS TO FRUSTRATE YOU SO YOU BUY MORE, first. How hard would it have been to not be that angry person and instead just come back to the table, cheery, so that people eat the food your girlfriend has spent THREE DAYS PREPARING, and no one is uncomfortable? How could he have so little regard for something I had worked so hard on and that had been so important to me?

But there are no answers. And I leave a spotless kitchen to sleep in the spare room alone so I can wake up fresh in the morning and write more jokes about why Kim Kardashian is a whore.

Tip

When You're Angry, the Kitchen Gets Clean. Just like anger fuels a workout, it can also fuel a good clean and those dishes for twelve aren't going to clean themselves. Plus, you'd be surprised how therapeutic it is when you feel like your life is a gigantic mess and you're incapable of doing anything right, to have a clean kitchen and see that at least you can put effort into something with positive results because clearly THE EFFORT I'M PUTTING INTO THIS RELATIONSHIP IS HAVING FUCK-ALL EFFECT!

Recipe
Braised Lamb Shank:
Not for the Gluten-Free

Ingredients

Olive oil

4 lamb shanks

3 tablespoons flour, plus more for dredging

Salt and pepper, or blackening spices to season

1 large onion, diced or sliced

2 tablespoons minced garlic

1 bottle red wine

1 quart beef broth

3 sprigs thyme

3 sprigs Italian or flat leaf parsley

1 bay leaf

2 tablespoons butter

Yield: 4 servings

AUTHOR'S NOTE: If you have a problem eating cute animals that often find their way onto the bibs of babies, you may want to skip this, with the knowledge that you are a much better person than I am. Seriously. No bullshit. I'm not mocking you. When I look at my cats, I feel very conflicted with the fact that I eat meat. That's usually when The Boyfriend reminds me that they eat meat. I also feel bad because I like to eat all of the cute animals: rabbits, pigeons, lamb, but could go the rest of my life without eating a cow. In the final analysis, I'm not sure my moral relativism makes much of a difference. Like I said, you are a stronger person than I.

You can buy one lamb shank per person if you choose. We do this because The Boyfriend says it looks nicer on the plate. However, I think that lamb shanks are usually a lot of meat for one person, and you can always split them up between people. If, like The Boyfriend, you want the Fred Flintstone aesthetics of a whole shank when you plate the food, you can always use the leftover meat in a stew the next day. It will be delicious.

Heat olive oil in a large Dutch oven or roaster. See? Your Le Creuset is really coming in handy. Dredge (that means roll around until coated) lamb shanks in seasoned flour. We like to use a little blackening spice, but you could use paprika, or just salt and pepper. You can omit the flour for people with gluten allergies.

Over medium high heat, sear each side of the lamb shank, until browned. Remove from the pot.

Brown a diced or sliced onion for about 5 to 10 minutes, add 2 tablespoons of garlic for 30 seconds, then red wine and beef stock or broth. You're going to want to have a bottle of wine and at least 1 quart of broth on hand, although you might not use all of it. I always try to add equal parts of both. You want to add just enough so that when you put the shanks back in they are almost covered, but not submerged. Also add to the mixture a couple of sprigs of thyme, maybe some Italian parsley. They always also say to add 1 bay leaf. Sure, add a bay leaf. I have no idea what flavor a bay leaf adds to any dish that I've ever prepared it with, but am often too afraid to leave it out. The good news is that they will keep in your fridge forever, which is about how long it is going to take you to go through a package of bay leaves.

Return the shanks to the pot. Adjust the liquid now if you need to. Leftover wine can be consumed by the chef while cooking.

Cover and simmer for 3 hours until the meat is tender and practically falling off the bone. Add more liquid if needed, but try not to drown your shanks, as you will have a harder time reducing your liquid.

When the lamb is done, you can remove the shanks and keep them warm in a covered dish. Now, chefs will use this opportunity to strain the braising liquid and then somehow reduce it all down to some thick, luscious sauce that has all the concentrated flavor of the lamb and not a bit of flour in it. Yay, chefs! You are magic. I however, am not. So I cheat, thickening with flour. Sometimes I just dissolve a few tablespoons in a cup of the braising juice and then add it all back in; other times, I use a buerre manié, a paste of 2 tablespoons butter, 3 tablespoons flour, adding it to the broth, stirring really fast while bringing it to a boil. Simmering it for 5 to 10 minutes after that should thicken it. Also, I don't strain. I have enough on my plate.

Serve each lamb shank on a plate of mushroom risotto.

Chapter 14
How to Throw a Dinner Party for 2 and Save Your Relationship

Kim was sick.

It had been a shameful almost eight months since we had seen her. We'd made these plans almost five weeks ago and now she was sick.

I had a sixth sense that this wasn't going to happen. After all, you don't not see someone for almost eight months because they have a great immune system and are reliable. So I had something of a backup plan in place the week leading up to my plans with Kim.

But then the backup plan fell through. And there we were, The Boyfriend and I, finding ourselves with a free Saturday night. A Saturday night where we had no plans and no one to spend it with . . . except each other.

What the hell were we going to do?

His first suggestion was a restaurant. Did we want to go out to dinner? Not really. It felt like it was all we did anymore. He was working close to seventy hours a week; we didn't even eat dinner together Monday through Thursday and Friday nights were unpredictable. He never knew if he'd get out in time for dinner so it was hard for me to work up the necessary amount of enthusiasm to cook a nice dinner for two when it was questionable whether or not there'd be a "two" when dinner was served. Usually what happened was that I would meet a friend out for an early evening wine tasting and The Boyfriend would try to swing by when he got off work. By the time we left happy hour at 8:00 or so, neither one of us felt like figuring out a menu, grocery shopping, and then cooking. It was just easier to go out. And we were frequently eating out on Saturdays, too. Only then it was the more formal plan. There was always another couple or two that we had plans with. Sometimes we cooked or they cooked, but just as much of the time we went out to a new restaurant someone wanted to try, an old favorite that we hadn't been to in a while, or a place that was halfway in between our geographically distant homes. Sometimes it was inevitable. We'd have plans with friends who, for reasons either practical or petty, we just couldn't cook for that weekend. Now what's the alternative? Am I going to invite myself over to their house and make them cook for me and my multitude of food allergies? Or am I going to take the social cue off their lack of an invite and say, "Let's go out to eat?"

The truth was, his seventy-hour workweek (plus my writing jokes about why Kim Kardashian is a whore) allowed us to try pretty much every restaurant we wanted to in LA on a regular basis. What had once been special had become pretty routine and I think we both had the good sense in that moment to not force ourselves to go out and order a $22 plate of pasta just because we didn't know what to do with ourselves when we were alone.

But what *were* we going to do with ourselves?

We had the night free and we had to eat. This much we knew. But what was the plan? And let me just say here that sometimes, as a couple, you don't want a plan. You want to hang out in yoga pants, read a book, and help yourself to whatever you can forage in your fridge, whenever you want to eat it. And if he wants to play that stupid Batman: Arkham City game for three straight hours, that's cool, too, because I'm the one who said I just wanted to hang out and read Anthony Bourdain's murder mystery.

But let me just say that if your plan is to have no plan, you need to plan that. That needs to be an agreed-upon plan for BOTH PARTIES. You don't want to be that person who, two hours into some catatonic Arkham City crime spree, finds out that your girlfriend thought you were going to spend the evening actually doing something together.

We were agreed that we needed a plan and that plan could not be a "no plan" evening. (Now you may be wondering here, why not just go to the movies? You may, in fact, have wondered that thirteen chapters ago. Why not just go to the movies with all of your friends, Tess, and be ten pounds lighter and have thousands of dollars that would be otherwise squandered on Italian wines and truffle honey, in the bank? All I can say is that I am a very difficult person to go to the movies with. I am endlessly picky about what I choose to see, I hate waiting in line, and I get incensed spending four dollars for a water. It's not like it's aged Gouda. Also, you can't talk to people and laugh and catch up during a movie and that was what I really craved during dinner.)

We needed a plan so the night didn't slip into something regrettable like watching *Another 48 Hours* on some cable channel even I had never heard of.

"We could cook . . ." The Boyfriend began.

For ourselves? Just us? No one else? Even I had to admit it was a novel idea. We cook for everyone else. Why not each other?

When we first got our house, we threw a big housewarming party. We probably invited eighty to a hundred people. It was a lot of work, further complicated by the fact that our wireless music system wasn't working that day, either. (Did it ever?) But we were excited; owning a house was still the American Dream and not just something you were financially underwater in. I think we both enjoyed the party, but the following weekend, we found ourselves throwing a second housewarming, just for each other. We sent each other an invitation, got dressed up, and even printed up a menu. We knew how to do a dinner party for two; we had just forgotten that we could.

"What do you want to cook . . . ?" I asked, poring through our treasured collection of cookbooks and recipes that it seemed we never had the time to look through anymore. The Boyfriend thought for a moment. "Well . . . we could do soufflés?"

Ever since we had had them at Liz and Jack's house, we had wondered how complicated they were and if we could do it, but had never had the time to try something new. And we certainly weren't going to try something new and potentially complicated when we were having guests over. That was reserved for something we already knew was complicated. But this was just us. We had the time and no one to impress. Cooking something different felt adventurous.

We quickly found a recipe and could now spend some time trying to find the right wine to serve. This was a treat, too. When serving wine to friends it's always a choice between want you want to drink, what you want to save, and what you think your guests might actually enjoy. Let's be honest, something too good might not get appreciated by your guests and you just might spend the whole night wishing you had hoarded it for yourself. Many a morning I've woken to the unfortunate reminder that I wasted a bottle I had been looking forward to enjoying, opening it last when everyone's palate was shot and no one finished their glasses.

But this was all for us. We could take five minutes to discuss the wine we thought would be best and enjoy it as it opened up and not worry that anyone was going to be tired of our pretentious bullshit. We settled on a Bordeaux, thinking a French wine was only appropriate for soufflés and the simple French lentil and shrimp salad we were serving with it.

But now came the test: could we make a soufflé? We followed the instructions, hoping we were letting the béchamel sauce cool just enough before adding the egg yolks. We beat the egg whites into stiff peaks, an intimidating job made easier with the help of the KitchenAid. In no time, we were pouring the batter into buttered ramekins and putting them into the oven, waiting to see what would happen.

They were fantastic! We were both amazed at our success and impressed by our own abilities when we took them out of the oven, puffy and slightly browned on top. They were light and airy inside, delicious but not filling. We toasted our food with our wine, the two things that started us on this journey together.

The truth was, entertaining for so many people had taken its toll on us. We didn't want to give up something that, under good circumstances, we really enjoyed. We just needed to remember what those good circumstances were: being able to laugh when a pizza falls on the ground; knowing that what seems like runny polenta to you will just seem like dinner to others; and always refusing medical-grade pot when it's offered. And most importantly we had to remind ourselves that while we love feeding others, it's just as important to nourish ourselves.

Driven as we constantly were to be extraordinary, that night we had actually found something extraordinary in the ordinary. We were just a couple having dinner together, after all. And no one had to be there to see it but us.

Tip

Treat each other like guests. Don't make them wait. Prepare a nice meal for them. Express interest in their opinions over dinner. Ask them if you can get them anything else. Refill their wineglasses. Make not just the nights when others come over special, but the nights when you're alone, too, because they are the most special of all.

Epilogue
How to Have a Wedding
Dinner for 12

All of a sudden, everything changed.

I was leaving my job, my home of nearly seven and a half years, *The Soup*. And I had decided to celebrate this exciting new phase of my life and/or potential financial ruin, by renting a house in Tuscany for a month with friends.

And suddenly it seemed like as good a time as any for The Boyfriend and I to get married.

I could bore you with a bunch of complicated and highly technical phrases like "potentially losing health insurance," or "cheaper than estate planning," but suffice it to say that when we made the decision about four weeks from my departure from my job and the country, we realized we had a rare opportunity to elope in Rome, a place that meant a lot to us as a couple. Where we had shared many wonderful times and amazing meals, and that it just so happened there would already be a few friends in town staying at a villa up the Autostrada.

A wedding is the ultimate dinner party. Things like runny polenta and uncooked turkey are mere amuse-bouches compared to the crises that can await you while planning and executing a wedding. One woman confessed to me that her father hadn't spoken to her since her wedding, **three years before!** We had heard the horror stories, we knew the pitfalls, and we wanted none of it. A wedding was the exact reason we had never had a wedding before! (Along with many other "exact reasons" too numerous to mention in this epilogue. That is fodder, Dear Reader, for another story.)

But we weren't having a usual wedding celebration. We were eloping. And all our years of driving ourselves and each other to new and complex psychotic breaks with our quest for elaborate dinner parties finally paid off: we made a reservation at a restaurant.

Ristorante Al Bric was always our favorite place in Rome, the restaurant we always went to on our first night in town. Within moments of deciding to elope I said, "And we'll take everyone to dinner afterward at Al Bric." Such was my desire to keep it simple that I refused every suggestion from The (Now) Fiancé that we should pick the menu. I wanted to do zero work and make zero decisions before this wedding besides making a reservation.

And it was perfect.

My quest to throw the perfect dinner party was realized that night in Rome. Everyone got along. Total strangers sat next to each other and told each other their life's stories, made each other laugh, and ate off each other's plates. And when the food came out... everyone paused as they tried their food and for each course there was that moment of silence as we savored that first bite and then banged our fists on the table and said, "Holy Christ, that's good!" ("Holy Christ" seeming only fitting as we were in such close proximity to the Vatican.) And the wine flowed: from the Prosecco before the ceremony near the Colosseum, to the Brunello with dinner, to my final image of the evening, gazing out our hotel window overlooking the Pantheon I saw Edie and Steve sitting on the steps of the fountain, splitting a bottle of wine with the best man, George, who they had first met twenty-four hours before. The Husband and I waved before we closed the shutters.

At some point during our four-hour dinner, Krysia, my maid of honor, made a toast.

"Over the years I've been lucky enough to come to their house for countless amazing meals. If you've been there on one of these occasions, you probably noticed that they are always cooking together—in sync. Thinking of this, it struck me that a good meal requires much of what a lasting marriage has: good ingredients, compromise, and teamwork."

Relationships *are* like a good meal; some nights they just don't come together right. People are late, sauces refuse to thicken, patience thins, and ovens refuse to heat while tempers flare. We start with the best of intentions, only to be disappointed when we fail to present our best efforts to the people whom we want to show our best to. But if the ingredients are good, if you forgive others as well as yourself, and if you learn to laugh about what goes wrong, you can have a surprisingly wonderful and magical time anyway. (And sometimes, you may find yourself getting married in Rome.) Just remember: the most important thing is that we're together.